Ukiyoto Publishing

All global publishing rights are held by

Ukiyoto Publishing

Published in 2024

Content Copyright © Ukiyoto

ISBN 9789362696380

All rights reserved.

No part of this publication may be reproduced, transmitted, or stored in a retrieval system, in any form by any means, electronic, mechanical, photocopying, recording or otherwise, without the prior permission of the publisher.

The moral rights of the author have been asserted.

This is a work of fiction. Names, characters, businesses, places, events, locales, and incidents are either the products of the author's imagination or used in a fictitious manner. Any resemblance to actual persons, living or dead, or actual events is purely coincidental.

This book is sold subject to the condition that it shall not by way of trade or otherwise, be lent, resold, hired out or otherwise circulated, without the publisher's prior consent, in any form of binding or cover other than that in which it is published.

www.ukiyoto.com

Contents

Short Story by Juju's Pearls (Dr. Reemanshu Bansal)	1
Poem by Riddhima Sen	14
Poem by Rhodesia	16
Story by Purnima Dixit	26
Story by Dr Yogesh A Gupta	31
Story by Sanjai Banerji	41
Short Story by Dr.Renuka K.P.	53
Story by Ishita Bagchi	70
Poem by Kamalika Bhattacharya	78
Story by Aurobindo Ghosh	88
Story by Sabbani Laxminarayana	106
Short Story by Romita Sahni	113
Short Story by Velmula Jayapal Reddy	121
About the Authors	*124*

Juju's Pearls

DR. REEMANSHU BANSAL

11'11'02 Wishes!

Prelude

Wish by definition is to feel or express a strong desire or hope for something that cannot or probably will not happen.

Wish is the most innate desire of every human being, a state of feeling incomplete, unhappy by just a margin. Many a times, we are enjoying and are in a happy state of mind, yet we often take a deep breath sigh and start by saying, "Oh! I wish…."

The beautiful aspect is wish comes from heart and not brain. Anything from heart is generally pure and filled with love. This is a primary need. However, when it turns into greed, none can say. There is a faint thin line between the pure wish and greed. Having circled this planet Earth, nearly five decades, I have had my share of happiness-sadness, success- failure, homecomings- goodbyes and so on. My heart has a list of many such wishes which I will write in numerical order.

Many of you may resonate with them. My writings are inked from my soul, written in simple language. My philosophy is, "If each one shares honestly, majority of life's problems will vanish. Issue is nobody dares to share authentically. Generally, they are sugar coated. Life is all about sharing and creating memories. But, pause! a word of caution-Be careful with whom you share, that's the whole crux."

I will give my readers a glimpse into my life and share my list of wishes in different age group of my life- past, future and present.

I have categorized my wishes into past, present and future. I will share my most important innate wish in last chapter 3, which will inspire everyone to believe a little more, to hope a little stronger, and to keep on wishing, because you never know when your dreams might come true.

Chapter 1

If I could travel back in time, I wish....

1. I could have stored my chocolates in a box rather than slide under the bed and almirahs. When we shifted our first house, my mother collected a huge pile of chocolates – untouched, partially eaten. This was an act by a three-year old mind to protect her chocolates from her siblings. Little mind never realized that she had wasted a good number of chocolates.

2. I could have let my elder sister sleep in front of the cooler in summers rather than putting up a fight every evening as to who will get more cool air. She was, rather is a noble soul who always obliged. Later my parents motivated her to take a stand and rotation system was started by my mother and everyone got a chance to sleep in front of cooler.

3. I wish I could have focussed more on my studies rather wasting time in playing with street urchins, learning their bad language and abuses. I was scolded by my mother so much but all fell on deaf ears. It was during one trip to Nainital, hill station in Uttarakhand, India, my mother told me to spit all the bad language in a paperback, tied it tightly

and threw from top of mountains. Since then, I have been very careful about my choice of words.

4. I wish I had changed my school after class tenth to DPS, RK Puram, New Delhi and not listened to our school Principal and my eldest sister.

5. I wish I should have gathered courage and auditioned for play by Barry John Sir who had come to our school to teach dramatics/theatre.

6. I wish I had taken individual fresh coaching for my medical entrance examinations and not relied on my sister's notes.

7. I wish I could counsel my maternal uncle to take my granny back. I was small and had a traumatic effect when I witnessed my uncle literally kicking my granny and dragging her out of the house, calling her by names. None of the onlookers interfered. Not even my mother. She just helped granny, collected her things and moved her into an old age home.

8. I wish I had the courage to take that middle-aged man in DTC bus who was constantly harassing me for the entire trip from Sreenivas Puri till Saket. I just kept quiet and ignored (as I had been taught) I was fifteen then and couldn't understand much as to what was happening.

9. I wish I had accepted the film offer by famous director Subhash Ghai while I was in my medical school. Life would have been so different. In those times, film industry had a bad name. He

persuaded me to come to Bombay (now Mumbai) for audition test and I repeatedly refused. He finally left by saying, 'Juju, the ball is in your court."

10. I wish I had accepted ad film offer too. I refused without even considering the terms and conditions. I had a choice to give dates for shoot as per my course schedule and I could have easily continued my studies.

11. I wish I had made one boyfriend, rode on bike with him. Though I had many proposals, I never encouraged anyone. I was very focussed rather stubborn.

Chapter 2

If I had the time machine to go into future ....

1. I wish for a small comfortable house with a library, cosy room on the bank of river Ganges.
2. I wish to do the Base camp of Mount Everest in coming year.
3. I wish to go to Kailash Man Sarovar pilgrimage.
4. I wish to go on a jungle retreat with my books and my kettle (for making tea/coffee)
5. I wish to go to Norway, lie on the ground and witness Northen Lights Aurora Borealis.
6. I wish to cross the Arctic circle by jumping over the line and getting a perfect click.
7. I wish to build an orphanage and old age home side by side. This will serve the dual purpose. Children will get elders and seniors won't feel lonely.
8. I wish to build a wildlife sanctuary for tigers. Elephants and chimpanzees.
9. I wish all human beings turn vegetarian and stop killing animals for food and other monetary benefits.
10. I wish all children living in slums start attending schools and pass their twelfth class at least if not a graduate qualification.

11. I wish for a world of gender equality where women are respected for who they are and not seen as inferior to men.

Chapter 3

My two most important wishes which I dare to wish and share is on professional front and other on my personal front.

Professional:

I wish I could have attempted my exam one more time before dropping it forever. Medical licensing exam Part 1 for United states of America. I vividly remember my result on that ill fateful day. I had missed by one mark. In our times, it was about getting a minimum required pass percentage. My teachers including my parents thought I was good in academics and would pass the exam. I had taken a break of three months from my internship and dedicated myself to studies. I read only the books and notes available. Seniors who were guiding had already passed their exam and suggested doing books and notes would suffice. I didn't take adequate number of practice tests to have a self-assessment. I realised it's importance much later.

I felt guilty about wasting my parent's money on my exam. In our times, one had to go abroad to take the exam. Singapore was the closest country after Thailand. After my result, I had decided to appear for home country post-graduation. God had better plans and I got residency in Radiology in Asia's premier institute -Tata Memorial Hospital, Mumbai.

I had good recommendations, grades and Uncle Sam was a dream life. I have vivid memories of receiving the envelope from the postman, gently tearing it open, pulling out a sheet, unfolding the result. And I went into a state of shock when my eyes saw inked in red, "Fail". This four-letter word had a profound effect on my soul that I went into traumatic shock. I just decided for myself that this dream was never going to come true and dropped it like a hot cake.

My parents counselled me to take the test again. I was adamant. My parents had put a condition and it was to get married and then go abroad. I wanted to see world through my own lens. I must have been in a very fragile state of mind at the age of a twenty-two year. I wish I had acted more sensibly, studied under guidance and taken up the exam. It would have been more than twenty-five years now living in my dream country.

My parents knew about my American dream. They gave a suggestion to get married to a boy from America and then take exam. Chances of clearing exam in home conditions always gives an edge. I was not willing to pay such a heavy price for my dream. So, my soul decided to shelve the idea. Now I feel this was a real bad idea, my biggest mistake. I wanted to do things my way.

This wish was neatly tucked deep inside my soul. It resurfaced when I got an email about this book. I felt as if numerous wishes got liberated from my subconscious mind. It took me nearly one whole day to figure out my two priority wishes.

Personal

The other wish is-

I wish I could have revived my mother from her death bed. There are so any things I want to share, talk about and show her, how well I am doing in my current life. She would have been so proud of me. Mother's love is unconditional and your mother is your biggest cheer leader. Her reassuring words were, "Don't worry Raju, God takes care of everything. Have faith and just keep on doing your work."

On that ill fateful day, she was seeking my help in altering turbans into stoles and scarves. I had already got some work done from market. And decided to do the pending work post lunch and evening tea. June 18th, 2015, time 4 pm, the most disturbing time in our life – My mother felt uncomfortable on lying down, spoke to my Intensivist sister and decided to shift her to Cardiac centre at the earliest. She left her mortal coil soon after. She went in a peaceful state. I remember her face so vividly. There was not a single frown or fear of death. She had embraced death as she had embraced life.

Things would have been much nicer. Ever since she left, the joy of going home –my Delhi has gone. It's more of a moral duty to visit my father, brother and his family. Everyone loves me and waits for my trip. Yet, my heart longs for that familiar smile and voice, "Hello Raju!"

I wish to hug her just one more time, to talk to her just one more time, to tell her about my daughter becoming a doctor and my son entering into medical school. She always blessed my children and said, "These two are future doctors."

Oh Maa! where have you gone?

My mind says, you are in a different realm from where you can watch us, hear us and bless us. It's a miserable feeling to yearn for that hug, touch and voice. It's going to be nine years now. My mind says, Goodbyes are always difficult and I have already crossed that difficult path. Do I really wish her alive?

Time will come to say good bye again, I don't want to go through same emotional turmoil all over again. Practically thinking, I feel I don't wish for anything in current juncture of my life. My life is beautiful as it is. Like my children say, "Maa! you have created a beautiful life."

Epilogue

However, I have many little wishes which I feel I could have corrected if I had the courage as written in Chapter 1. Few wishes are on my bucket list, which I have written in Chapter 2. If I had to write about my most important wishes, I have written in chapter 3. That's the title of my story 11'11'02.

The list is endless. Wishes come from heart time and again. At times, these seem like dreams or goals rather than wishes, especially the ones I have mentioned about future.

Past cannot be undone and the yearning will remain till my last breadth. Nobody has seen the future, it's mystic. The only moment we have is of present.

Happy reading! Happy wishing. Most important is to live and love in present, enjoy life NOW.

Riddhima Sen

Hues of Mundanity

Colourful hues beaming through the horizon,
Eloquent tints of turquoise blue;
Tigered with shades of baby pink,
And tinged with hues of exuberance,
Spread all across the sky.

These are the hues of mundanity,
The insignia of daily activities,
Abounding in sorrow, yet
The smell of coffee emerging from the ceramic table,
The much acquainted fabric of the cotton t-shirts
With words   that motivate
Are mundane yet precious.

Rhodesia

Yesterday

This day last year,
I was broke,
I was jobless,
And trapped in a culture
That didn't allow me to work.

I had a ten-year mortgage,
Insurance plans,
Car maintenance,
Installments on credit card,
And two kids to support.

I was confined in a marriage
Of lashful words,
Hurtful looks,
And tempered violence,
Where fear and confusion reigned.

I was publicly mocked,
Laughed at,
An outcast
Of a society I have served
With all my strength, soul and heart.

What should I have done?
Should I hope?

Make a Wish

Should I wish?
Where would I go?
Did anybody care to know?

Today

I celebrate my solar return -
Afloat on a river
Driving a pink kayak,
While relishing soothing music
Under azure skies and alabaster clouds.

My kids live the good life -
Glamping under the stars,
Soaking in the cool pool,
Groomed in a fine school,
Loved, and never lacking anything.

Just recently, I was elated
To be granted citations
Of international recognition,
Just doing the missions
Freely flowing from my bosom.

Everyday I touch lives,
Heal their malady
And ease their pain,
While taking care of my family
From the comfort of home.

All because one day,
I whispered my wishes,

My agonies and pleas,
To Someone who listens,
Defends, saves, grants, and sees.

Tomorrow

What is there anything else to wish
After the dragons are tamed
And the demons slaughtered?
When the tormentors and oppressors
Invoke to amend and be friends?

A lot, for they share no portion
In my tunnel of vision,
Except to be forgiven,
Expressed gratitude and smile on
For being released from their dominion.

This day next year,
I will continue to enlighten,
And melt hearts across the globe,
Instilling life in written words,
Reviving someone else's lost hope.

My patients will be blessed
With the warmth of my care,
And the seasoned familiarity
Of all ailments and their cure,
Restoring their zest and vigor.

My children will grow
Stronger, healthier, and happier

Loved, supported and protected,
Guided to the ultimate fulfillment
Of their best version imagined.

Thereafter

There will come a time
When I will go further
And no one will hinder,
To places I have not been,
And cultures I have not seen.

My clan will fructify
Like a sturdy evergreen
That can surpass seasons,
Gifting humankind
With their rare contribution.

I shall leave legacies
In the schools and facilities
I toiled to establish,
And with divine intelligence
I will guide the sovereigns.

I will reach a century,
And not succumb to frailty,
But with grace and beauty,
I will inspire many
To take good care of the body.

I will be cherished,
And fiercely loved,

Someone will hold my hand,
And we will never part,
Until the end of time.

Epilogue

I now pass this torch
To open hearts and souls
That in their struggles,
May they continue to hope
Trust, believe, and cope.

May the wishes they whisper
In a cold, dark, night,
And the longings they've kept
In the recesses of their hearts
Be brought to life.

Purnima Dixit

Wishes are Dream come True

"**S**ia Do you accept Ryan Adams as your husband??" She excitedly **said yes** making every guest at wedding smile at her cuteness. Closing her eyes she was awaiting her husband to kiss her, and whole room clapped and cheered for newly wedded couple, when she felt someone shaking her, she tried her best to ignore it, but she woke up with a start as she felt her duvet being pulled off and she felt the chills of December month.

Sia gave an annoyed look to her mom, as she broke her dream "He was about to kiss me, Mom" her mother laughed her antics, this dream girl always dreams about her crush on Ryan, her best friend & their next-door neighbor. Her daughter has only one WISH ever since she met Ryan, "**To be Ryan's wife**"

Mother just shook her head, as she asked her to get ready for office left her room not before commenting, "Your wish will not come true if you keep sleeping, you will have to work for it darling"

++++

Sia smiled to heherself, only if Mom knows, how much hard she is working for her Wish to come true only if that dumbo thinks about anything beyond his dancing, he wants to be a professional dancer. Only she knows how many direct hints she had tried to give Ryan, sending him flowers, gifts, love notes...still that dork can't understand her feelings, just keeps fooling around. Her only relief is, since he is so clueless about love and dating, he can't see other girls falling for his handsomeness and charms. He simply doesn't realize how girls fall for him when he is on stage, he is one of the most sought for performers in their college.

++++

Ryan excitedly looked at the door for the fifth time as he has something important to share with his best friend Sia.

Just thinking about her made him smile, Sia his best friend, since childhood, since he knew meaning of friends, they have literally grown up together. Their group of friends have name them inseparables...as they are always together. Not only did they attend the same schools, and virtually had the same group of friends, they shared a unique bond, where they could just understand each other well, **they shared all their secrets about friends, books they read, movies, their thoughts everything.** And it's not he could not understand all hints thrown by Sia, that she is head over heels love with him, he could read the fondness, the smitten expression in her eyes.

He also loves her infact **he had been madly in love with Sia, since the moment he had first set eyes**

on her, when their family had moved next door. He always wants to see her happy, be there for her, only he knows how much he wanted to confess the very first time he realised his feelings but before that he wanted to achieve his goal of being a professional dancer, he had promised himself he would confess when he achieved that dream and today he did...He had been selected as main dancer with International Dance Academy.

Carefully hiding Sia's gift in his hand behind his back he patiently waits for her.

+++

Sia gaped as she saw Ryan kneeling down on one knee and presenting her the ring and expectantly looking at her, with all their friends cheering them up...She is confused if this happening for real or she is still in her dream which she sees everyday.... Ryan's words still ringing in her ears...

I know I have nothing to give you right now, but I can promise You have all of me and all of my Heart, all my Love, all my Smiles...only for you!! I belong to You and I see our future together. (Joked) You are the one who make my heart dance, Be the music to my Life and I can dance to your beats forever with You.

Will you be partner till the end??

Sia eyes brimmed with happy tears...she has accepted him as love of her long back and she didn't took a second to say **YES** to this dreamy proposal...She hugged him as Ryan engulfed her in his arms...twirling away with happiness & his World in his arms he was in heaven.

They were about to leave the Christmas party, when their friends stopped them cheering both of them to Kiss, Both Ryan and Sia gave them confused looks, but their friends pointed to look up to see where they were standing.

As an astonished Ryan looked up at the ceiling, he saw a huge red and green mistletoe hanging there, he knows the tradition any couple who stands under mistletoe has to kiss.... Sia looked up to Ryan as his chocolate brown eyes seemed to melt into her very soul as he came forward, and the entire room plunged in silence as he held her close leaving a light kiss on lips.

The whole room roared with clapping, congratulating the "just-in-love couple".

As Sia looked down at the sparkling solitaire on her ring finger, she felt like her Dream literally came true. She had always dreamt of this day.

Who said, Dreams don't come true....Her forever WISH has come true like a Dream!!!!

Dr. Yogesh A. Gupta

Eleven Eleven: A Girl's Wish for Courage and the Lessons That Echo Through Time

In the bustling streets of a middle-class neighborhood, where the echoes of children' laughter intertwine with the rhythm of everyday life, lies the tale of a young girl named Arayna. At nine years old, she navigates the complexities of friendship, courage, and standing up for what's right in a world where bullies lurk in school corridors and society playgrounds alike.

Arayna's story unfolds against the backdrop of her ordinary yet vibrant life, filled with the simple joys of family, school, and play. But beneath the surface, she grapples with a profound understanding gleaned from the stories she loves—mythology, history, and her cherished TV show, "Chhota Bheem." Through these tales, Arayna learns the timeless lessons of loyalty and bravery, lessons that will soon be put to the test.

When Arayna discovers the power of making wishes on 11:11, she embarks on a journey of self-discovery and resilience. Faced with the plight of her friend Vamika, who endures relentless bullying, Arayna summons the courage to stand up against injustice, drawing inspiration from the heroes of her imagination.

As Arayna's wish unfolds, her actions ripple through her community, igniting a spark of solidarity among her peers and challenging the status quo. Through her unwavering determination and unwavering belief in the power of friendship, Arayna proves that even the smallest voice can spark monumental change.

In the pages that follow, join Arayna on her quest to defy expectations, challenge bullies, and champion the bonds of friendship. For in her story lies a timeless reminder that courage knows no bounds and that standing up for what's right can change the world, one wish at a time.

***

Arayna is a middle class family girl who is 9 year old. She has an elder sister Manya. They both live with their parents. Daily they get up and go to school and return back by afternoon and by evening goes to badminton and chess. They come back and then do their homework and if no work then play with their friend downside. By night they come back eat their dinner and then may be watch TV for a while and then sleep. This was their routine.

Arayna was an avid reader of books and she liked different kinds of books, mythology, history, fiction, comics,and many more. She also like watching her favorite TV show Chotta Bheem. From this stories as well as Chotta Bheem and his friends Chutki, Raju,

Kaliya and all she had learnt one thing. She undertood that friends are most important people after family. And that one should always stand for the friends. She has seen how Krishna stood for Sudama, Rama stood for Sugreev, Chotta Bheem stood for each of his friends. But somehow she lacked that courage. She easily got panicked if someone bullied her in society play ground or even in school. While playing in society there were parents who used to shout on kids and interfere between kids. In need of protecting their own child they shouted on other kids and so kids always felt disturbed. In school there were parents who kept pushing their kids for every events and in doing so forced teachers to not allow other kids. Because of this many kids out of arrogance used to bully other kids.

While watching Chotta Bheem one day Arayna saw how Bheem wished from Krishna power to fight evil

Aryana asked her dad about wish and making it. She was amused about the science and truth behind that. Her dad told her about 11.11 make a wish. She was really surprised by this. So she thought of doing that. Come 11.11 and she wished. She actually made a wish for her friend Vamika. Vamika was harrassed by other kids. They did not allow her to participate in any events of school. They laughed at her as she was very studious. They make fun of her for being slow in sports. Arayna did not like this attitude of other kids. She saw her friend crying one day. So when she heard about this make a wish, she decided to ask to God or whosoever is going to fulfil this wish that she be granted courage and strength to stand against this bullying kids for her friend.

After making that wish she went to school next day. But then she saw Vamika was absent in school. She felt sad. She went through her routine that day. But then this was repeated for next 10 days. She was now very sad and she asked her teacher about Vamika. Teacher told that she was sick and so was not coming. Arayna then went home and ask her mother to ring Vamika's mother to inquire about her health. Her mother called Vamika's mother. She said Vamika was crying all days as she felt bad because of bully by other kids and that she want to change the school

Arayna came to know about this. Now she was angry. Vamika came to school after few days. Seeing her Arayna was very happy. She met her and she sat with her in same bench that day. In lunch they talked with each other and shared their tiffin. Suddenly the kids who bullied Vamika came and started making fun of her.

One kid:" So we heard you were sick. What happened? By being ill you should have become slower.

Another kid: No no she would loose ranking this time as she could not study.

Another kid said: We were so happy not seeing you all this day. We could easily get into various culture events posted next week.

Another kid: Arayna you should stop talking to her otherwise we will punish you. We will complain against you to teacher

Now Aryana was very angry. Suddenly she had surge of courage and strength. All this days of not seeing Vamika, hearing about her ordeal, her crying and possibility of her leaving the school made her very angry. She stood up and shouted

"How dare you speak such a way to my friend? Don't you dare?

The kids got bit scared looking into Aryana's eyes

She continued: She is the best student of the school. Not like you who keeps copying in exams

She said: Even her homework's are always finished, she helps other kids. You all are lazy people

One of the kid came forward to push Arayna. Arayna catches her hand and pushed her back. She said: Don't you dare. I will complain to my mom and she will then complain to principal.

Another kid shouted: We will make your life hell. Let's see how you get into any events

Arayna said: Really. You get into events through your mom. They are always forcing teachers. They don't allow you to grow your abilities. You will be losers when you grow up

Vamiki was surprised to see such scenes. She was feeling very happy that her friend was standing for her.

Arayna finally said. : I am warning you all. Keep away from Vamiki and me.

Seeing this scenes other kids who also like Vamiki and Arayna but were fearful of this bullying kids came around. They also stood with Arayna and defended both. Now the bullying kids show more kids on other side. Now they feared and they ran away.

Vamiki was very happy and she hugged Arayna. She cried and said now she will not have to change the school.

Arayna while returning back understood the meaning of wish.

She though whether she got courage from wish or not but when you see that you will lose someone who you love a lot or like a lot then you get courage. She also understood that when you stand for right then other also will come to stand with you.

Now was the time to go to the society playground. Arayna's heart pounded as she approached the society playground, where shadows of past confrontations lurked in every corner. With each step, her resolve hardened, fueled by a mixture of fear and determination. Today, she would no longer be a silent bystander to the bullies who roamed the playground like predators.

As she entered the playground, whispers and glances followed her every move. The familiar knot of anxiety tightened in her stomach, but she pushed it aside, steeling herself for the confrontation ahead. With her chin held high, Arayna approached the group of kids who had made her playground visits a living nightmare.

Keshav, Risika, Rashmi, and Rishi, the ringleaders of the bullies, stood with smirks on their faces, ready to unleash their barrage of insults.

"You again?" Keshav sneered, his voice dripping with disdain. "You need to learn to stay away from us by now."

Risika chimed in, her laughter shrill and mocking. "What's the matter, Arayna? Can't handle a little teasing?"

Arayna felt a surge of anger rising within her, but she fought to keep her composure. She had learned from her stories that true strength lay in restraint, not retaliation.

As the bullying continued, Arayna stood her ground, refusing to give her tormentors the satisfaction of seeing her crumble. But just as she thought she could endure no more, a new challenge emerged.

The mothers of Keshav, Risika, Rashmi, and Rishi appeared on the scene, their faces twisted in anger as they berated Arayna and the other children.

"Arayna, how dare you speak back to my child?" Keshav's mother scolded, her voice sharp and accusatory. "You should be ashamed of yourself!"

Arayna felt a pang of fear as the mothers closed in, their words like daggers aimed at her fragile resolve.

But she refused to back down, meeting their accusations with a steely gaze and a quiet determination.

"I will not apologize for standing up for what is right," Arayna said, her voice calm but firm. "Your children's behavior is unacceptable, and I will not tolerate it any longer."

With grace and discipline, Arayna faced down her tormentors, refusing to be intimidated by their words or their anger. And as the sun set on the playground, casting long shadows across the scene of their confrontation, Arayna walked away with her head held high.

As Arayna grew older, the lessons of courage, standing up for oneself, and standing up for friends remained etched in her heart, guiding her through the challenges and triumphs of life. With each passing year, her understanding of the power of wishes deepened, and she learned to wield them wisely, knowing that they held the potential to shape not only her own destiny but also the world around her.

Armed with the strength she had gained from standing up to bullies and defending her friends, Arayna navigated the complexities of adolescence with grace and resilience. When faced with difficult decisions or moments of doubt, she drew upon the lessons of her youth, trusting in her instincts and remaining true to her principles.

As she embarked on her journey into adulthood, Arayna's belief in the importance of making wishes for the right reasons only strengthened. She understood that wishes were not mere whims or fantasies but powerful manifestations of one's deepest desires and aspirations. With each wish she made, Arayna sought to bring about positive change, whether for herself, her loved ones, or her community.

Through her unwavering commitment to standing up for what was right and her belief in the transformative power of wishes, Arayna became a beacon of hope and inspiration to those around her. Her courage, integrity, and compassion touched the lives of many, leaving a lasting legacy of kindness and empowerment for generations to come.

In the end, Arayna's journey was not just about overcoming obstacles or achieving personal success; it was about using her voice and her wishes to make the world a better place for all. And as she looked back on her life, she knew that every wish she had made, every challenge she had faced, and every lesson she had learned had brought her closer to fulfilling her greatest wish of all—to make a positive impact on the world and leave behind a legacy of love, courage, and hope.

Sanjai Banerji

A Journey of Friendship and Triumph

"What the heck?" Shourya said to Acharya, seated beside him. "We both received pathetic appraisals. Are we that incapable?"

Both sat under the Bodhi Tree in the Stupa area of Sanchi, a small town renowned for its ancient Buddhist site, a UNESCO World Heritage site.

"We old fogies have got a raw deal. Management wants young, bright Newtons with amazingly high IQ levels. Our brains are getting redundant. Top Management wants us out. No Fogies. Only Bright Newtons, is their mantra," berated Acharya without pausing for breath.

Shourya chided Acharya, "If I say your IQ level matches mine, don't take it as a compliment." Both laughed, but Acharya began to cough. Shourya thumped Acharya's back. "Old man, you've got to quit smoking. There's no point kicking the bucket before our tenure is over."

"Top Management is an asshole. They will screw us anyway," replied Acharya, staring nonchalantly at his muddy shoes. "Got to get my boots cleaned. Have a presentation with the MD next week. We're both fifty-five now. What's your plan?"

"Training for an ultra-marathon in three months in Jaisalmer. The race is 80 kilometers. Cut-off timing is 12 hours," Shourya replied with bravado.

"I knew you were nutty, but you just confirmed it. You've been running marathons for the past three years. What's the reason for the upgrade? Are you tired of living?"

"Want to live my passion now. I don't care a fuck for my jealous Boss and corporate politics bordering on nepotism," Shourya replied with firmness, belying his sophomoric mind.

Both watched the setting sun sink over the hemispherical dome adorned with intricate carvings depicting stories from Buddha's life until stars illuminated the sky. Then, after sharing a *Cadbury Almond Roasted Bar*, they got up, arms over each other's shoulders, and reached the tourist taxi at the parking lot. They planned to reach Bhopal within two hours, have dinner there, and then proceed by train to their Plant at Satna to reach the office by 8 a.m. the next morning.

During dinner, their usual bickering took place.

"What's the point of being a vegetarian when you need animal protein to sustain your brain? The only other reason your BP gets high is that you don't eat mutton, chicken, fish, and eggs," Shourya remarked.

Acharya, annoyed, replied with a nonchalant wave of the hand. "Shourya, you need meat to run. I don't. You admitted at Sanchi that your IQ matches mine. So what's the big deal with being a devout veggie? In fact, I am planning to up the ante to become a pure vegan."

Shourya, in an expatriating tone, got up. "Are you crazy, old man? Being vegan means you can't have any milk products and also animal byproducts like honey. Imagine a world without milk, ghee, and honey. No more barfi, rasagullas, ice cream, milkshakes, or dosas with ghee. I am going to tell Ritu that you flipped."

"Acharya quipped, "Ritu is collaborating, Bro."

Shourya sat down and replied, "At least both of you crazy coots will keep each other company."

Midnight Running

Shourya punched out sharply at 5 pm on Saturday, had early dinner of chicken stew, buttered toasted bread, and a glass of orange juice. Thank God, Golu supported his ultra-marathon training. The alarm rang shrilly, and Golu nudged him awake. Shourya got up, made his way to the dining room, where Golu had placed his pre-run meal on the table the previous night. A packet of sucrose gels, three electrolyte tetra packs, chocolate, a bottle of Strawberry Flavored Milk, a few cans of Coca-Cola, caffeine strips, peanut butter sandwiches, and a container of salt tablets. Shourya brushed his teeth, munched some chocolates, drank strawberry milk, and finished a tetra pack of electrolytes. He observed his two-liter hydration backpack filled and ready. A small yellow sticker fluttered at the top. It read 'All the best for tonight's run. Lots of Love, Golu.' Shourya smiled and got ready with the rest of his preparation for the 8-hour midnight run in their company campus, which had a 5-kilometer loop.

Shourya planned to do 12 loops totaling 60 kilometers. After massaging his legs, donning his gear, and filling his hydration pack, Shourya got into his Honda City. It was only a five-minute drive from his house to the 5K road inside the Housing Colony.

Starting his Garmin, which showed 12:15 am, Shourya ran under the starry sky with the scent of jasmine flowers reaching his nostrils. The April warmth comforted Shaurya as he took sips of water from his hydration pack. A security jeep patrolling the colony waved to Shourya, who waved back. The path ahead was lonely, but determination drove the 55-year-old. A red Hibiscus flower fell on his head, and Shaurya took it as a sign of blessing.

By 5:30 am, the first group of early morning walkers greeted Shaurya. Even after five and a half hours, Shaurya maintained his pace, diligently using salt tablets to prevent cramps. At the end of eight hours, Shaurya beamed with pride. He had completed 63 kilometers against his goal of 60 kilometers! It was an awesome Sunday morning.

Workplace Ethos

Shaurya strode into Acharya's cabin with a swagger and a plan, which made Acharya almost fall off his chair.

"Old man, how would you like to do a Basic Mountaineering Course? Nobody's done it at an age beyond 55 years. I am 58 now. MD has sanctioned my expenses for the 29-day course from Atal Bihari

Vaypayee Institute of Mountaineering and Allied Sports," said Shaurya smiling.

Acharya stood up, made a bow, and did a Namaste. He then came out in front of his table and hugged Shaurya. "You are one helluva Dude, Shaurya. You never cease to amaze me." Acharya called out to his department colleagues. "You guys come here. Shaurya has done the incredible."

After the accolades, the crowd dispersed, and both Shaurya and Acharya huddled together.

"Buddy, I have an ambitious plan. I complete the course in July next month. After my return, we make groundwork to scale the highest point of the African Continent, Mount Kilimanjaro, Uhuru Peak at 5895 meters. Eight-day program, we both will do it."

A bewildered Acharya replied, "You crazy Dude, I can't even do five pushups. My belly is protruding. Never even ran one kilometer in my life. No way can I survive up there. Heard the oxygen level is 40 percent less than at sea level. You can do it easily, Shaurya, but count me out."

Shaurya replied, "Acharya, I will give you a training program, which will prepare you to run a 10K race within three months. It's a 90-day foolproof program I designed for people like you." Both laughed heartily.

After the banter, Acharya out of breath stated, "Sorry Shaurya, I will never be able to pull it off, but you got the tenacity to summit. All the best."

"Thank you, Acharya. Now let's study the report Boss sent us in the morning. He will be expecting a reply tomorrow itself."

Acharya gave a terse reply, "Yes, the Rascal will be baying for blood for sure. Let's sit down and work on it."

Shaurya sprinted to his cabin and returned with his laptop. Both crunched numbers on the software. Acharya, after an hour, gave a disdained statement with a peeved look on his face. "Rascal is going to screw us tomorrow if our figures don't match his report."

"Old man, take a walk on the porch outside and return in half an hour. I will make sure the figures match," replied Shaurya.

"You are a genius man. Can't match algorithms the way you do. Running enhanced your brain for sure."

Shaurya ruminated, "What a messed up life I am leading. Was made for incredible stuff. Working in a shit hole with a jealous Boss."

Acharya replied, "At least we get our salary on time with annual increments, Shaurya."

Shaurya silently nodded his head in agreement.

The Kilimanjaro Challenge

Shaurya looked at the breakfast table at Horombo Hut before him. Boiled eggs, bananas, avocados, porridge, bread toast, and chicken sausages. A call came through. It was Acharya.

"Shaurya, where the hell are you? Can't you at least make a phone call to Golu? She's worried for you like the rest of us. Even MD phoned me up to inquire. She told me to tell you, if you have any medical issues climbing to the summit, to return. She will still reimburse all your expenses."

Shaurya, in his usual cheerful self, replied, "Acharya, old man. Tell Golu I am fine. Not to worry. The weather is not very good. It's difficult to catch the tower here. All mobile networks are down. Tell MD not to worry. Going for the summit push in two days. Wish you were with me, Acharya."

"Take care, Dude," replied Acharya, and the network got cut off.

The trek to Kibo Hut took seven hours. Shaurya looked at the dark clouds looming ahead and discussed with the team leader, Colonel Ranveer Singh.

"Good to see you looking so sprightly at 59. Our teammates are not so good. Out of ten, two have stayed back at Horombo Hut and will fly back home. At Kibo, three are already suffering from high altitude sickness. So, Shaurya, there will be five from the team for the final summit, including me."

"Colonel Ranveer, let's hope for the best," replied Shaurya.

The final summit climb from Kibo Hut was a disaster from the beginning. It began raining heavily, and pebbles and rocks slid down. Colonel called to his team to get behind the ridge to avoid an avalanche. As the group settled down behind the ridge, there was light snowfall. They halted for half an hour until it stopped.

"Okay, guys, we need to head for Gilman Point and reach by sunrise," said Colonel. Shaurya adjusted the height of the trekking poles and continued climbing. At Gilman Point, two more climbers suffered from high altitude sickness and decided to withdraw. Shaurya looked at Colonel Ranveer and Anita, the sole woman colleague, a 54-year-old professor from Delhi University.

"Are you game, Anita?" Shaurya asked.

"What are we waiting for? Let's move towards Stella Point. From there, it will be only 200 meters to the summit," replied Anita unwaveringly.

As they approached the summit, a snowstorm hit, reducing visibility. After two hours, the skies cleared, and the trio reached the summit, exhausted, but jubilant. They take photos and sang the national anthem.

Meeting with the MD

Shaurya and Acharya sat outside MD's cabin. Acharya remarked, "I am sure Rascal Boss complained about us, and that's why we are summoned just three months before our retirement. The Rascal does not want us to complete our tenure."

Shaurya extended his arm and squeezed Acharya's shoulders. "We should never challenge our destiny, old man. God is always protecting the innocent. Incidentally, we were not summoned by MD. HR requested us to meet her."

MD's secretary entered and pointed to both Shaurya and Acharya. "You both are next, after your Boss comes out."

Acharya panicked, "Shit, Shaurya, we didn't know this. Rascal Boss was called today before us by MD. We are going to lose our jobs for sure."

The secretary noticed Acharya's sweating face. "Are you feeling okay, Mr. Acharya? Can I get you something?"

Shaurya intervened, "He is just worried about his retirement plans, which are due next year. Don't worry, Acharya. It will be all right."

Shaurya entered MD's cabin with Acharya in tow. MD, a no-nonsense woman, observed the duo from behind her oval-shaped table. "Please be seated, Mr. Shaurya and Mr. Acharya," she stated sternly.

Shaurya took the initiative. "Good afternoon, Madam. We were told you wanted to meet us regarding some important matter."

MD's face softened, and she leaned back in her chair. "Shaurya and Acharya, you both are one of the oldest employees in this Plant. Your tenure here has been commendable. You have maintained discipline, productivity, and have kept your teams motivated. We are thankful for your service."

Shaurya and Acharya exchanged perplexed looks. Acharya stammered, "But Madam, we thought…"

MD cut him off, "Yes, I understand. You were probably concerned about your retirement. But I assure you, this meeting is not about your termination. It's about something quite different."

She paused for a moment and then continued, "We are planning to open a new division focusing on environmental sustainability and corporate social responsibility. We need experienced individuals like you to lead this initiative. Would you both be interested?"

Shaurya and Acharya were dumbfounded. After a moment of silence, Shaurya managed to say, "Madam, we are deeply honored. We will definitely give our best to this new endeavor."

MD smiled, "That's settled then. You will receive the detailed proposal by tomorrow. I trust you both to handle this responsibility efficiently."

As they exited MD's cabin, Acharya turned to Shaurya, "What just happened?"

Shaurya chuckled, "Looks like our luck turned, old man. Let's embrace this new challenge together."

Acharya nodded, a smile creeping onto his face, "Indeed, Shaurya Let's conquer this new summit."

Epilogue

Golu was ecstatic when Shaurya and Acharya narrated their meeting with MD to her. She hugged Shaurya tightly, tears streaming down her cheeks. "I'm so proud of you, Shaurya," she said, planting a kiss on his forehead.

Acharya's wife, Ritu, was equally jubilant. "I always knew you had it in you, Acharya," she said, beaming with pride.

Shaurya and Acharya continued their corporate journey, now leading the new division on environmental sustainability with zeal and dedication. Their friendship, forged over decades, only grew stronger with each passing challenge they faced together.

As the sun set behind the Bodhi Tree in Sanchi, Shaurya and Acharya sat once again, reminiscing about their journey and contemplating the peaks they had yet to conquer. But this time, they knew they were ready for whatever challenges lay ahead, armed with the strength of their friendship and the resilience of their spirits.

And so, their saga continued, a testament to the indomitable human spirit and the power of camaraderie to overcome any obstacle in life's tumultuous journey.

Renuka KP

Divine Order

Once upon a time, there lived two teenagers named Sarah and Jack in a small town nestled between small hills and small streams. They were neighbors, played together, grew up, and went to school. Their friendship develops deeper as they navigate through the anxieties and travails of adolescence together because a boy entering adolescence is usually less likely to be handsome or capable. His voice may not be beautiful and he may be unwanted by anyone. At that age when the voice itself starts to change, it is the love and care of the parents that they can often survive the situations. But unfortunately, Jack's mother left them and lives in another town. Jack lives with his father and sometimes when he says something seriously, he is ridiculed as if he did not hear such a small child talking like this. If he talks like a child, he will be scolded saying that such a big boy is talking like a child. How pitiful is the story of Patik Chakraborty, who succumbed to the tragic end without getting love and care at this age? But his playmate Sarah, who has almost matured at this same age, is the support and solace for him today. Her presence and care were enough to relieve his mental stress. Because Sara is an intelligent child who can think and act independently. Sara had tried to understand his stresses and find a solution. Her laughter was like a chime in the wind.

With bright eyes the color of the clear sky and a smile that could light up even the darkest nights, she was the beacon of joy in Jack's life. On the other hand, Jack was very quiet and kept to himself and tried to put his pains and troubles on the pages of books. In all such cases, her presence gave him a life and color.

And so their companionship was moving towards innocent love. Their every word and look filled with love made even their classrooms more radiant. They were weaving their life each other, sharing dreams, and exchanging promises.They spent the spring wandering in the woods there, chasing the stars in the sky, sharing their hopes and longings in the evenings. Every moment spent together made them feel like a precious gift, a treasure to be kept forever. So one day, while walking around the valley, Jack asked

"Do you know what my favorite thing in the world is?"
Sarah: "What?"

Jack: "To look the sparkle in your eyes when you laugh."
Sarah: "Sometimes I wonder if it's all a dream."
Jack: "If that's the case, may we never wake up. I want to live with you forever in this dream."

Sarah: "Do you believe in fate?"

Jack: "I trust us. That's enough."

Sarah:"If I could, I would make my feelings as a poem"

Jack: "Then I would have sung it. Sarah, my love for you is beyond words."

Sarah: "Sometimes I'm afraid our bond won't last forever." Jack: "Don't be afraid, my love, I'll be with you in any situation. Together we'll face all." Sarah: "You are mine forever. Wherever you are, I am there."

Sarah and Jack have been together since childhood. Jack's father, who was serious and strict, loved her very much. They enjoyed her presence in that motherless house. If they didn't see her one day, they would panic. Growing up together in that small town, Jack and Sarah's lives were intertwined like the branches of an old oak tree. Their laughter as they shared secrets and dreams echoed through the streets like the melody of a familiar song.

However, fate is not always kind to those lovers who wish their life should be. As they entered high school, cracks began to form in their innocent relationship. Beset by financial problems, Jack's family made a painful decision to move to a bustling city in search of better opportunities. He is going to be isolated from everything he knew and loved, including his beloved Sarah, and moved to another place on the other side of the country. Fate became cruel to them just as life turned towards adolescence and love. This news shocked Sarah and Jack like a thunderbolt. Jack couldn't do anything about it and could only watch helplessly. Their lives were thrown into a sea of uncertainty as a question mark. The news shattered their dreams of a future together, and they cling to each other, vowing to overcome the odds and maintain their relationship no matter where the world ends up. They walked hand in hand under the stars for several nights, trying to capture each other's facial expressions and voices, their souls themselves.. And so one fateful night, under the cover of darkness in a canopy of stars, Sarah and Jack met for the last time. Tears flowed from their eyes as they embraced, oblivious to each other's surroundings, their hearts heaving with the weight of unspoken journeys. They parted with aching hearts wrapped in smiles and began their journey along their separate ways. Although the cruel hands of fate shattered their love, they believed that the memories they shared would last forever.

A reminder of a beautiful and fleeting love. As they move on to new paths, they join in the hope that this time will pass and their love will be rekindled in the light of a new dawn.

But as the days passed and the date of departure approached, an emptiness began to overwhelm them like a thick fog. They knew that no matter how much they wanted to, they would soon be torn apart by forces beyond their control. The final days were filled with bitter tearful farewells and their hearts were aching every second. Breaking the silence Jack said

Jack: "We'll see each other again."

Sarah: "I'm scared when I think about our separation."

Jack: "Yes, how long can we hold out?"

Sarah: "Are you saying... to break up?"

Jack: "But it's time to accept that things have changed."

Sarah: "But Jack, I love you..this separation feels like a part of me is missing."

Jack: "I know, it hurts me too."

Sarah: "I wish we could return to our old lives."

Jack: "Me too Sarah. Maybe this is the start of something new for both of us."

Sarah: "You may be right. I will always treasure the time we spent together in the corner of my heart."

Jack: "Me too. You'll always have a special place in my heart. Don't I have you in my heart?"

And then, that day came. Standing on the platform of the railway station, Sarah and Jack hugged each other, their tears mixed with the soft sobs of the rain. As the train pulls away, carrying Jack to an uncertain future, Sarah feels like a piece of her soul is being ripped out. That night, Sara couldn't sleep alone in her room and cried. Painful memories of a life without Jack by her side haunted her dreams. Days turned into weeks, then months, but the pain in her heart refused to go away. It was increasing.

Despite the distance, Sarah and Jack tried to stay in touch through letters and phone calls, but the void left by their separation remains unbridgeable. Slowly, the intensity of their love began to wane with the necessity of time. With a heavy heart, they realize that they are not the same people they were once deeply in love with. Jack slowly adjusts to new situations. He starts working with his father. New people, new relationships. Although he always cherished the moments they shared, he also realized that some things, no matter how much he wanted them, could not last.

But as the days passed, the pain of separation began to intensify for Sarah. Jack's letters and phone calls became less. It was unbearable for her. She tried to hold on to the joyous and intermittent silences in his conversations, clinging to the memories of their past. But the distance between them began to grow too large to overcome.

By the heaviness of uncertainty, her heart was heavily weighed down and life was dragging on. One day, when the clock struck 11:11, she was standing by the window with heartache. Suddenly, she felt a sense. She folded her hands to her chest and prayed to the universe. She closed her eyes and asked for help from the universe to get her old Jack back and live with him. She imagined that she could repair her lost relationship with Jack and that they would live together again. And she didn't try to remember Jack after sending her wish to the universe.

The next day, while walking through the city street, lost in thought, Sarah felt a tap on her shoulder. Her breath caught in her throat when she turned around to see Jack standing behind her, with a soft smile on his lips.

"Sarah," he called. His voice was mixed with longing and regret, "I thought a lot about our lives. I miss you, I've missed the good times we both had together." He said regretfully.

Seeing the sincerity in Jack's gaze, tears flowed from Sarah's eyes. Without saying anything, she wrapped her arms around him and hugged him passionately. His hug felt like a life-giving touch.

Later she shared her grievances and frustrations. They went for long walks talking about everything for hours. They realized once again how much they loved each other.

Sarah and Jack worked tirelessly to rekindle their lost love. They laughed and shared their hopes and anxieties again, they revealed to each other the depth of their love in their hearts.

As the days turned into weeks and the weeks into months, Sarah and Jack fell in love again, deeper and more passionately than ever before. They forgave each other's faults and cherished every moment they spent together. When they walked hand in hand, Sara saw the sunset filling the sky with orange and pink colors, and Sarah believed her wish had come true.

Because she learned that with Jack's love, even the deepest wounds can heal and that love can conquer all. Sara and Jack walked talking on the bank of the wild stream or among the woods. One day Jack asked, "I was afraid of approaching you, I feared whether you would accept me."

Sarah: I was thinking about you all the time.
Jack: "My luck."

Sara: "I'm willing to do anything as long as we're together."
Jack: "Me too Sarah. I love you."

Sarah: "I love you too, Jack forever."

Jack: "We need to rebuild our lives as soon as possible."

Sarah: "If we stay together, we can achieve anything." Hearing that, Jack looked at her lovingly. Their reunion was the realization of honest and intense desire. Even nature was happy to see their will to overcome any difficulties together......

So far Lakshmi was reading an English storybook that Rahul had brought and given to her. After reading the story, Lakshmi suddenly felt confident. Till this time she was highly desperate as Rahul had not been calling or talking like he used to for some time. What is wrong with my Rahul? Is he in another relationship? The more she thought about it, the more upset she was...

Since her childhood, everyone had said that Lakshmi is for Rahul. But at that, time she could not understand the meaning of it and later when they grew old they realized the fact. Their ancestral home was an old nalukettu showing their heritage. They had owned a lot of landed property, and business firms under their control. They were under the supervision of her uncles who were dwelling in different homes near their tharavadu in a single compound. Grandmother had often said that Lakshmi is for Rahul only and had decided to marry Lakshmi to Rahul to keep the properties within the family members under their control. Lakshmi sings well and has studied dance and classical music. How nice it is to listen to her good keertanams with her mother at the time of Sandhyavandanam. Her hobby is singing along with other sisters from the courtyard of Nalukett or when she used to come to Kulakadav or Sarpakavu to light the lamp. Sometimes Rahul also comes to listen to Lakshmi's songs. It is in the same compound where he is residing. Playing the harp to the crow and the cat, singing against the song of the spotted sparrow, going into the room and reading books, or drawing something when feeling angry, sad, etc are her nature.. She was their ringleader when they were young. so they grew up like brothers, and Rahul gives many books to Lakshmi, who reads well.

After graduation, Lakshmi started studying fashion design. By that time, Rahul had to leave business and go to Europe for higher education in marketing. Rahul was not very interested in going, but the growth of the family business was their aim and had to be fulfilled. Until that day, they lived like brothers in a family house, and for the first time, they felt love. They began to meet secretly in the empty corridors, in Sarpakava, Kulakadavu, and Thodi. The news reached grandma's ears. They said that the children cannot be left like this for much longer. Once his studies are over, he should immediately take Lakshmi by the hand.

So when he flew to the UK, at first he used to call and talk to her frequently. There were few private conversations on mobile phones in that family home. That's why Rahul could not say much. Later, the call gradually decreased. Lakshmi spent her days thinking of Rahul in her heart.

At that time, her grandmother suddenly became ill. After a few days of treatment, Grandma died. Then Rahul came home to attend the funeral. He didn't show any love towards her as before. A strangeness. On the one hand, the sorrow of her grandma's departure. On the other hand, his negligence. All this time she was meditating for him. But when he came what was happening! now he doesn't even notice her. Then she calmed down thinking that it may be the presence of all family members now here. Still, She was hurt in her mind. She mostly confined herself to her room with the books given by Rahul. She doesn't want to take a bath or eat. However, she did everything automatically to avoid the attention of others. She wanted him to tell her why he was behaving like this. She began to cry without seeing anyone there. He is deliberately trying to avoid her. Lakshmi's mother Sridevi understood her distress. But she didn't say anything. She likes Rahul very much and it is also her mother's wish. Neither her brothers nor their wives are against this matter. After Rahul left, Grandma had discussed it with everyone. But what is the reason for the change in Rahul's expression? Lakshmi's mother also began to worry. Sridevi wanted to talk about it to her Valyetan, the elder brother. But she had not talked about any serious things with Valyetan until now. Her mother had done everything. Sridevi's husband is also not with them now. They are a family that follows our cultural heritage strictly.

To protect a family, division of labor and specialization have been implemented since old times. When a man starts a family after marriage, he will have to earn an income by doing whatever the work he gets. He is liable to earn for the family by doing any work and live. He has been given a strong body to do any work all day no matter what work. After finishing his work in the evening, he would buy all the necessary things for the house at dusk. By that time, his intelligent and efficient wife would wake up at dawn, clean the house and its surroundings, cook for the family, and train their children to lead a dharmic life. Under the shadow of her mother's intelligence, love, and care, the children would grow up well and not be a burden to society.

By that time, it was misconstrued that 'na sthree swathandramarhathi'. Women were driven out of their homes saying that a woman's life is not meant to be confined to the four walls of the kitchen and sent the woman away. The domination of some reckless and unwise men paved the way for it also. With that, her intelligence and strength, which were only used for her family, were released to the outside world. Although all the old bonds of the houses were gone, she reached the top. Thus, when she gained independence, the great idea of our family was lost with all that mutual care and disintegrated. The relationship between husband and wife became like a contract. Those who completed the contract became rare. Children growing up alone without the care and shade of their father and mother and their silent pains on the one hand, marriage, and divorce, and one person having three or four marriages became common here. What can we say? This society is like a flying kite. It is quite unaware that when and where it will go and stick its nose.

In any case, Lakshmi's ancestral house is well-established. Her father is often traveling for business purposes. One day after Rahul went back, Sridevi told Valyetan about it. That's when she knows that there is another girl in UK who is behind him and she likes him. She knows Lakshmi is keeping all her dreams inside. She told her daughter slowly and understood the situation. She didn't say anything. She got into the world of her books. She thought that if her grandma had been there, how she would have been worried?

Although uncle and aunty like her, they changed their decision because she also works at their son's workplace. Moreover, they had not promised anything to Lakshmi. Rahul had got stuck in the magic of the modern world!

So when she was reading books desperate, she got the storybook of Jack and Sarah. She started to read that book and was inspired. At the time 11:11 Sarah is praying and bringing her Jack back into her life. How wonderful! if she prayed, her Rahul would also come back, she thought. He was so good. Someone must have cheated him. She knew that a foreign girl was following him. She wanted to save him from her. She waited for the night. At the time 11:11 came, she held both her hands together and prayed intensely. 'Oh God, Oh Universe, please listen that my Rahul does not fall for any woman's deception. Please give me back my Rahul.' She put both her hands to her heart and prayed inwardly. Along with it she imagined that the girl was leaving Rahul breaking their relationship and coming back to her. She felt Rahul apologizing to her for neglecting her. 'Oh Lord of the Universe, Oh god, please fulfill my wish.' She gave her wish to the universe and then slept soundly.

The next day started as normal. After the chores, she went to the kitchen and helped her mother and the maids. Later, when she is in her room, her mobile phone begins to ring. She picked up the phone. It was Rahul! She couldn't believe it. Her prayers worked. When he came here, he tried to avoid her. Now?

"Hello Hello Lakshmi."

"Hello Rahul."

"Did you forget me?"

"Do you think I can do so?" Then she shared all her cares and worries to him.

"I apologize to you, I was in another relationship and I kept quiet so as not to upset you."

"I understand."

"Now what happened to that relationship?"

"She relates to many people like me. Lakshmi, I miss you now I was worried about you."

"Maybe she needs everybody's help "

"Not so, it's a hobby for her to hook up with everyone."

"It doesn't matter, Rahul, you will still have a place in my heart. We grew up together, didn't you?"

"Will your parents not be sad now?"

"I didn't tell them. I told them not to think about anything else. They like you, but when I told them that I have another relationship, they just nodded."

"Don't worry. I don't want you to see you worried."

"Lakshmi, there is no obstacle between us. just tell me that you gave me pardon."

"Please be peaceful."

"Of course, I will call later" I was worried about how I tell you this. how merciful you are! How stupid I would have been to go after her."

"No matter what happens, I won't leave you. I want you,"
At the reunion, they realized the strength of their love. Perhaps this incident cemented their love. In any case, the universe has hidden anything good in any evil.

Lakshmi thought a lot. Reading is imparting knowledge. As we read each book, what things open up before us? It is books that opened this vast cosmic world in front of us. The open thoughts of others, the good and evil in society, the wisdom to join the good and leave the bad, everything is being received in reading. Through reading, we can see in imagination, opening our third eye. But there is no need for imagination in visual media.

However, now Lakshmi's happiness knows no bounds. She realizes that a small English story has changed her life. The cosmic power recognizes our desires and prepares words to achieve them. Hai, thank you universe, hai thank you the Lord of the universe! She again thanked the book, the storyteller who wrote it, and all the things she had done till she got it. Then she went to her mother and told her everything that had happened.

11:11 She was amazed to think how effective it was. When she told her mother everything and saw her daughter was happy, her mother also thanked the Universal Power for listening to her daughter's prayer. Lakshmi too, if she has a very strong desire, still prays and achieves it. At that time the universe will take over our intense desire, that is certain.

Ishita Bagchi

Bloom

I love flowers.

I really do.

Lilies,

Roses,

Sunflowers,

Orchids,

Chrysanthemums.

I love them all.

But I pressured myself not to love them for the longest time.

I pressured myself to pretend I was too cool to be fond of them.

Because the first time I said I loved flowers

And how sweet it would be to receive them from someone,

My bullies told me girls like me shouldn't be fond of flowers.

They said,

"Girls like me shouldn't be dreaming of love letters and flowers.

Girls like me, who are not pretty, don't receive flowers."

But the rebel in me wanted to shut them up.
The voice in me kept screaming internally,
"So what if no one gives me flowers?
I will buy them for myself.
So what if no one understands my wishes?
I will fulfill them on my own."
But I couldn't say it out loud.
I couldn't muster the courage to shut them up.
All that I could manage was a meek reply saying,
"I would just buy those."

"Ah! What a pity," they mocked.
"Well, that's what girls like you do.
Covering up your wishes with the facade of self-love,"
And once again, my bullies won, I thought.

But years later,
When I passed by a flower shop,

I stopped by to look at those fresh water-sprinkled flowers waiting to be packed.

I immediately picked one

And realized how much I loved them.

That day,

I bought one for myself,

Breaking one shackle at a time.

I felt free.

I felt that after so many years,

Even without trying,

I could finally find my old love for flowers coming back,

One day at a time.

And that, my friends, is how I fell in love with flowers,

All over again.

Holding On

Somedays, you don't know where

And whom to go to with all the grief that you hold.

Somedays, you don't know how to not beat yourself up

For feeling too much.

And on those days,

You keep fumbling in the darkness for a hand to reach out to,

For someone to hold you,

Unconditionally.

On those days,

You just wish someone would be there for you,

No questions asked,

No terms and conditions applied.

But on some days,

When you have no one to go to,

You become that person for yourself.

You hold yourself,

And keep believing you can fix it on your own,

Just like you could every other time.

I wish for a love like Eleanor & Park

When I first read "Eleanor and Park" by Rainbow Russell, their love felt like a rollercoaster of intense and raw emotions yet full of innocence.

Finding a love like Eleanor and Park's may not be about replicating their story but instead seeking a genuine and deep connection with someone who accepts and understands you for who you are. And here's what I had written as an 18-year-old naive kid based on my understanding of what Eleanor and Park's story meant to me.

If there's anything worth all the nightmares and storms,

Then don't let it go

Just for the fear of breaking down.

Life might try to turn your smile might turn into a frown

But darling, if it is something you want

Then nurture it and hold on with all your might.

The world might tell you that all of this happens only in fairytales

But don't give up if you think what you want is right.

But when I read the book again a few months back, I realized how naive and idealistic I was in perceiving love. And then I also realized that it hasn't changed even after all the heartbreaks and losses. I still am that stupid 18-year-old naive kid when it comes to love. I will still cross oceans for people without a second thought or expecting them to even cross a puddle for me. I will still stay up late being anxious and worrying about the person I love if I don't receive an update about them the entire day. Some things just don't change, I guess. Some things are so innately intertwined with our nature that no matter how harsh the world gets, they just don't go away.

I still long for the moments I have read in the books while growing up.

I still long for the moments I have romanticised while reading my favourite poems.

Long phone calls about anything and everything under the sun.

Laughing at the lamest jokes.

Picking up the phone to let me know about the most insignificant things and making me feel like I am a part of their life.

Long hugs when we meet.

Holding hands and not letting it go even when palms get sweaty.

Being their designated person when something goes downhill and they need motivation.

Waking them up in the morning when you promised to do so.

Sharing your favourite songs even when they might have heard them before a thousand times.

Remembering little things about them, from their favourite ice cream flavour to their pet peeves.

I long for moments like these which I have romanticised since time immemorial.

Kamalika Bhattacharya

Wish

Just a thought,

If I have a last minute to wish upon,

I would like to pray that,

 when the next person calls you charming,

does in a way that encompasses all of you..

When they find you exquisite,

they mean your voice in the morning is as bright as a beam of sunlight,

and yet lit in the light of your eyes like twilight...

I hope when they admire you,

they see what you are passionate about,

hope they will find you adorable,

when you will sneeze and suddenly your nose will turn pink,

I hope they will find you cute,

even if you forget your keys everytime before you leave,

so you always say goodbye twice before you leave for work,

I hope they will like you the way you sleep,

the way you walk, the way you drink your coffee...

... Because next time nothing about you should remain disregarded..

And all this while I only tried to reach you with my words,

but it's not easy to love....

When I revisit my love notes for you

i see how gullible I am and scared of the fact

that you will fade away...

and again my soul will be empty.

I apologize for being so clingy...

but I will never regret loving you madly.

However, the door to my heart remains ajar,

And I can't deny of having

Endless fandom for you,

The simple reason of all of it is love…

No matter what...

Silent Storm

There is an overgrown tree near my place,

It stands as witness to my melancholy

Of moods, its huge size and open branches

often look at me as if they want to wrap me in its arms and tell,

so what things are not how you want them to be...

your heart is enticed by someones shadow who's not picture perfect either,

and yet you accept the love it brings...

We all learn to dance with devils,

Somewhere along the way to heaven....

You are not an fallen angel,

But yet everything about you feels flawless,

Your truth, your words, your being.

Even the parts you cast away...

Everytime my eyes became teary,

The universe knows something,

It knows i needed your light,

From sun to midnight...

And yet I remained hollow,
You never returned.

I don't mind kissing your insecurities...
The layers of love you offered never hurt,
because i learned to accept you in every way,
to look at you with love...
We fill our eyes with love to marvel at our beloved..
Like creepers trying to match their hands,
You are woven into each fiber
of my soul deep within..

Spot it!

You are the laughter that
echoes in the corridors of my heart,
 In the silence of nights,
when I ride the chariots of yesterday,
I am crowded by your memories,
 That distinct fragrance of yours.
My fingers still remember the   meadows of your face,
Those timeless curves of your lips,
And that tranquillity of
Your face...

Listen my love,
I want to remember you,
Long after the silverfish
would have eaten my youthfulness,
I want to recall your face,
the spark of your eyes,
the echoes of your voice calling out my name,
the crook of your arms,

the clasp of your hands on mine,
The arch of your dreams,
I barged into,
the butterflies of our first kiss,
The turbulence of my heart
When I surrendered

The light of that moment when we became US,
The wet pillowcases and my trembling lips
Uttering your name,
The pain of the tattoo inking our love,

A gaze of yours meeting mine,
 Those silent pillow talks we shared,
Those lazy moments in each others arms,
 Those bundle of love we know we have,
Those colours of sorrow we always hide,
That parting of hands when we said goodbye,
I want to remember you, A little longer than,
Your memory allows you to.
Just spot it and keep it safe.

Wordshore

I want to grew up as a kind hearted person, With sheer good intentions and no Expectations,

With less anxiety, and more divinity,

With less of blockage and more of forbearance.

With less disapproval and more solicitousness. With less of hurt and more of gentleness.

With less of barbarousness and more of thoughtfulness.

With less selfishness and more graciousness. With less of harshness and more of tolerance,

With less cruelty and affection.

With less of a disadvantage and more of benevolence.

With less meanness and more charity.

With less of obstruction and more of magnanimity.

With less of hindrance and more of clemency.

With less hostility and more acceptance.

With less of indecency and more of beneficence.'

With less animosity and more tenderness.

With less of injury and more of succor.
With less pride and more amiability.
With less resentment and more assistance.
With less prejudice and more helpfulness.

With less of impasse and more of considerations.
With less of foulness and more of goodness.
With less of outrageousness and more of indulgence.
With less of coarseness and more of altruism.
With less of vileness and more of temperance.

With less of offense and more of endurance.
With less of greed and more of qualms.
With less of malice and more of regard.
With less of beastliness and more of compassion.

With less of covetousness and more of agreement.
With less of wickedness and more of responsiveness.
With less of pettiness and more of warmheartedness.
With less of unworthiness and more of affinity.

With less of apathy and more of generosity.
With less of detachment and more of bounty,
With less of listlessness and more of forgiveness.'
With less of disdain and more of humanity.
With undivided love and unparalleled feelings

Let's grow in eachother, for eachother.

Aurobindo Ghosh

Bimladadi's Dream

Kantilal's son Shantilal was very small when his mother Pramila died. Kantilal's mother Bimladadi found the situation quite difficult for her to handle. Kantilal would go to open his grocery shop by 6.30 in the morning. He used to have breakfast with tea when his wife was alive as well as carry his tiffin box for lunch as the shop was quite far and it was not possible to come home in the afternoon. He would generally comeback home by almost 9pm when everybody in the house would be waiting for him to have dinner together. But now, the situation was different. Shantilal was very attached to his grandmother, Bimladadi. While taking care of her grandson, it was not possible to look after her son Kantilal's early morning breakfast and prepare the tiffin for lunch. Shantilal was only three years old when his mother passed away. He did not know what death is. Bimladadi told him that his mother had gone far away. It would take time for her to come back. The small boy always wondered why his mother went alone and did not take him with her. Often, he would ask Bimladadi about his mother and would insist to go to his mother. Finding no solution to all the problems which cropped up after the demise of Pramila, Bimladadi confronted her son Kantilal one Sunday, "Look beta, it is true that my daughter in law

Pramila was a very nice girl. When she was there, I was free to look after my grandson Shantilal. Pramila was then able to look after you. We all were happy. But now with Pramila no more with us, I am finding it very difficult to raise my loving grandson Shantilal because I have to devote more time for other chores of the house."

Kantilal knew the difficulties. But he too had no solution. He simply said to his mother, "Mother, I know with how much pain you are struggling to run this broken family. But what can I do, mother? I am helpless too."

Bimladadi was waiting for this opportunity to share her thoughts with her son; she said to Kantilal, "Listen carefully,I have a suggestion. It is almost six months now since Pramila left us. I can't face Shantilal anymore. He insisted on going to his mother. I don't have any answer. So, my suggestion to you is you should remarry. It would solve all the problems. Shantilal will get his new mother, you will get your new wife and this family will get a new caretaker. In that situation, I can look after Shantilal better than now. Very soon he will join school also. Somebody will be needed to drop him to his school too. So please seriously think about my suggestion. If you say yes, I will inform our neighbor Tulsibhabhi. She was asking about you. She has a good-looking niece. They are from the nearby village. There is no harm in seeing that girl. They know everything about us including Shantilal. Actually, that girl is very unfortunate. Five years back, her marriage was fixed. But timely the girl's family discovered that the boy had a girlfriend. Because of fear, he had kept it hidden. Just before marriage, the girlfriend's family arrived and revealed everything. The boy also confessed that he loved his girlfriend. The marriage broke right away. Unfortunately, everybody started saying that this girl was a 'bad omen'. For the last five years, that family has been trying hard to get their daughter married but no groom's family was ready to marry that girl. Perhaps no one will ever marry her. That poor girl perhaps will never get married without any fault of her own. If you marry her, she will remain grateful to you and she will love this family from the bottom of her heart. Tulsibhabhi said they would keep all your demands. But I had already said, we have only one demand and that is Shantilal must get his mother's love back. That was all we wanted."

It was a really big narration. Kantilal was confused. He knew his family needed a female member who would take care of this family. But he was not ready for this situation. There is a girl nearby, who is branded as 'bad omen' without her fault. Nobody is ready to marry her for unknown reasons. Kantilal was really upset about the so-called social beliefs. Rather he was angry.

"OK mother, I am ready to see that girl. But I have a condition. Let her prove that she could take care of your grandson Shantilal, only then I will go ahead with your suggestion. But not before that I shall listen to anything. Is that ok with you?" Kantilal concluded.

Bimladadi was very happy. She just asked, "For that, what do I have to do and what would that girl have to do?"

Kantilal said, "Simple. Ask Tulsibhabhi to bring her niece to her, you take Shantilal to their house, give them time to be acquainted, let the girl befriend the child. Don't hurry. Give them sufficient time. Remember mother, if at all I listen to your suggestion, I shall marry only for the betterment of Shantilal and not mine. If Shantilal is ready to accept the girl as his new mother, I shall do whatever you say. But if I find the Shantilal has reservations regarding accepting that girl as his new mother, then please do not pressurize me to remarry."

Bimladadi was very glad. Atleast her son had agreed to her proposal to think about his remarriage which he had sidelined from his agenda. Next day, early in the morning, she went to her neighbor Tulsibhabhi and asked her to bring her niece as quickly as possible. Before Tulsibhabhi could react to her untimely appearance,she narrated the conversation that took place between her and her son Kantilal. Tulsibhabhi became excited to hear the good news. Tulsibhabhi assured her that she would bring her niece to her home. After greetings, Bimladadi departed and Tulsibhabhi went inside to get ready to go to her brother's place to give the good news to her brother.

Accordingly, Tulsibhabhi reached her brother's place the same afternoon. Before she entered the house she shouted, "Banno beta, where are you? See who has come." Her niece Banno was busy in the kitchen cleaning the utensils gathered after the family lunch. All of a sudden, she heard Tulsibhabhi's voice calling her name. She immediately washed her hands, left all the remaining utensils as they were and started running towards the main gate. By the time she reached the main gate, she found that both her parents had already reached there and were welcoming Tulsibhabhi. Tulsibhabhi, being the eldest of the family and her father being her younger brother, all were busy touching the feet of Tulsibhabhi. And then she saw Banno, coming running towards her. Tulsibhabhi too started walking towards Banno her favorite niece whom she loved most. Both saw each other for a moment and hugged each other. Tulsibhabhi kissed the forehead of Banno and murmured, "Perhaps God had changed His mind and was ready to change your life."

Banno did not understand a word of Tulsibhabhi and looked at her inquisitively. Tulsibhabhi kept mum and with a hand gesture called everyone inside the room. Banno, her parents, her grandparents and Tulsibhabhi took their respective seats, and everyone waited for Tulsibhabhi to start.She looked to the ceiling with folded hand and started, "See here, sometime back, during my last visit here, I had a discussion with all the elders here except my child Banno. I told you that there is a boy who runs a grocery shop, who has recently lost his wife leaving him with an only child. The child is a boy who is just three years old. He is always searching for his mother. He is restless. Their family needs somebody who can take care of that boy as his true friend. Since last month, I was trying to convince the mother of that man, Bimladadi, about the remarriage of her son Kantilal. With great persuasion, the boy is ready to get married again, with a condition." Tulsibhabhi stopped her narration abruptly. As Banno was listening for the first time, she could partially guess that they were all discussing something about her. But she was sure that they could not be discussing about her marriage, which they had stopped considering, because of her being branded as a "Bad Omen Girl" in the society. She knew that her fate was already sealed and no person on this earth would ever take the risk of their lives by challenging the social norms. So, when Tulsibhabhi ultimately revealed the condition that if the child accepts somebody as his new mother, only then the child's father would be ready to marry that girl. Banno started both smiling and weeping on the inside. She was smiling about her fate which was compelling her to remarry a man with a child of three years and moreover had to prove to be a good mother of somebody else's child even before marriage. She was weeping as all her family members were so worried for her that they were ready to accept any damn condition, just to see her happy in life. She felt so helpless. Why does a girl have to suffer so much? But she decided to accept the challenge. With her handkerchief she wiped both her eyes and decided to take part in the discussion wholeheartedly.

Banno looked towards her grandparents and said, "Listen Dadaji and Dadiji, I know you are not in a position to say either yes or no. As the proposal brought by aunty is of remarriage, naturally you are confused. Let me make it easier. You all had arranged my marriage five years ago. But for some reasons, it could not materialize. Now let us suppose that we would have come to know that the boy was in a relationship with another woman after marriage. At that time, divorce would have been the only solution. Which would mean today I would have remained as a divorced woman. Now please analyze the situation with justification and sensibility. You would all agree with me that the present status of mine is a thousand times better than the brand of a divorced woman. So let me say something to you all. Let us give this opportunity a chance. See here, my justification is, if I try and be successful to have a real friendship with the little one, then by that time, I will come to know the entire family. It will be then our turn to decide whether to go ahead with the proposal. As there is no time limit, I think I should accept the challenge with your blessings and proceed."

Everybody was almost shocked after listening to Banno. They thought what a brave girl we have in our family! Nobody could utter a word. All were just staring towards 'Banno the bravo'. Banno realized that she herself had to take initiative. She wanted to give some relief to her family members from continuous agony. They had already suffered a lot. She was determined to find a solution. She thought about the worst possibility. She might fail in befriending the little boy and the marriage proposal would be terminated. But still, she would not repent of not trying. If she would wholeheartedly and sincerely try, the probability of her success would be quite high.

"Well, don't be so surprised." Banno continued. "Let us be rational. Let me go with aunty. Let us meet that family. Let me meet that little child a few times along with his family members. Let me be exclusively with the child, which may be difficult. But we must persist until the child is comfortable with me. Don't worry. If you all agree then tomorrow morning I shall go with aunty." All were very happy and gave their blessings to Banno for her adventurous journey which would decide her fate. Perhaps the Almighty was smiling from above.

Next day, early morning, both Banno and her aunty were ready to move. All family members were at the gate to bid farewell to both. Banno's mother was weeping and continuously calling her deity and asking her to give success to her unfortunate daughter, for assigning herself a very difficult activity. They both started for their destination. God knows why, on the way, Banno purchased some chocolates. By afternoon, they reached the village. After freshening up, they had their lunch which had been sent along by

Banno's mother. Tulsibhabhi asked Banno to get some rest as she would go to inform Bimladadi about their arrival. Banno knew that she would hardly sleep. She could hear the sound of her thumping heart. After her aunt's departure, Banno closed the gate and came to her bedroom. There was a mirror on the wall. She stood in front of the mirror. She looked at her face carefully. She was known to be the most beautiful girl at her school. She tried to find her charm in the mirror but failed. She felt herself robbed by that unknown person who, by breaking off the marriage, had inflicted on her a grievous wound throughout her being. She could not locate the earlier charming Banno. All she found was a mutilated,broken, and smashed Banno who was worthless and good for nothing. She shouted aloud and started weeping vigorously. She heard the knock at the front door. Hurriedly, she controlled herself, wiped her tears and came out to see something for which she was not prepared. An old lady with a smiling face was standing outside the gate with her aunty. Between them, a sweet little cute boy was standing. His hands were held by both the ladies. Before anything could be said by Banno to welcome them, the little boy jumped, freed himself from both the ladies, came running towards Banno and said, "Are you the angel, who my Dadi said will be my best friend?" He raised both his hands gesturing towards her to pick him up. Banno,on impulse,picked up the little boy and held him, hugging with both hands.

She said, "Yes, I am that angel who will be your best friend. We shall play many games together. I shall make toys for you. I know many songs. I shall sing for you. By the way, do you like chocolates?"

The charming boy nodded affirmatively. Banno took the boy inside the room to give him chocolates she had bought earlier unknowingly. She even forgot to introduce herself to Bimladadi. Tulsibhabhi brought Bimladadi inside. There were tears in the eyes of Bimladadi. They were tears of happiness. She immediately knew she had gotten what she wanted most. She could find a true companion in that girl for her grandchild and her son as well. Inside the room, on the bed there were two entities unknown to each other, by sheer faith in each other, laughing and talking and eating chocolates. When Bimladadi peeped into the room, she was astonished to see something which turned her head. Banno was lying on the bed with a pillow under her head and the little one was sitting right on her belly and laughing, talking in his innocent words with a chocolate in his hand. Bimladadi started sobbing. For the first time in six months the child was laughing as if he had got his mother back. No way could she waste any time. She had to do something before it was late. Bimladadi forgot the time. It was only an hour that the boy had gotten acquainted with Banno. It was surely a miracle. Even Banno could not believe the situation. She had given herself a couple of weeks to get close to the boy. But it seems God had different plans for her. Within one hour they were behaving like old buddies.

Like mother and son! Banno's motherly instinct had made this possible. When pure souls meet, miracles do happen. After some time, both Bimladadi and Tulsibhabhi came inside the room. Banno got up quickly and took the boy in her lap. She apologized to Bimladadi and said, "The boy is so cute that I simply got carried away. I am so sorry that I did not even bow down to touch your feet aunty. I do not know his name too. I have already kept a name for him. I shall call him as 'Chimpu'. Is that ok with you, aunty?" Bimladadi was so overwhelmed by the sweet gesture of Banno that she simply nodded affirmatively.

It was time for Bimladadi to go home, as Kantilal was supposed to come early today. But Shantilal was not ready to go. He wanted to be with Banno, his fairy friend. Satisfied with the promise of bringing Shantilal, alias Chimpu, to his fairy friend the next morning, he agreed to go home with Bimladadi. Back home, as soon as Shantilal saw his father, who was sitting on the sofa, he came running to Kantilal and jumped on his lap and excitedly started narrating the entire episode of his new fairy friend. Kantilal did not know anything. So, he looked towards his mother Bimladadi. There was a question mark in his eyes. Bimladadi came near to her son and told him everything in detail, of how Tulsibhabhi had convinced her family to make her niece ready to try to be a friend with Shantilal. She also described how quickly the girl Banno had managed to become a close friend of Shantilal. Banno even named this kid Chimpu. How sweet!

"Now son, I have a request for you. Please don't deny it. Let us invite Banno to our house for lunch tomorrow afternoon along with her aunty Tulsibhabhi. It will be nice if you and Banno get acquainted with each other. Let both of you know each other. That poor girl is also a sufferer of the social stigma with no fault of hers whatsoever. Both of you should give a chance to your respective lives. God has given us this opportunity to help each other. If you feel that Banno can be a true caretaker of your son, and she is equally competent to take charge of this family, then you marry her. If you feel otherwise, then we shall inform them accordingly. Moreover, Banno too should get equal opportunity to know all of us to decide about this relationship. She too has an equal right to do so." Bimladadi expressed her own feelings to her son.

Kantilal saw his son. For the first time in six months, Shantilal was not weeping for his lost mother. Perhaps he had found motherly love in Banno, whom he called fairy friend. Kantilal said to his mother, "Ok. I don't have any problem if you feel right; go ahead with your plan. Call her family for lunch tomorrow."

Next morning, Bimladadi took her grandson Chimpu (She too had started calling him Chimpu) to Banno. Banno was cleaning the floor of the verandah. As soon as she saw Chimpu along with Bimladadi, she hurriedly washed her hands and ran towards Chimpu and took him in her arms. She kissed his forehead, took a spin, and started talking. Chimpu had a lot many things to report to his fairy friend. His father had brought a red colored car which could run very fast. Bimladadi was very happy to see that, within a day, they had become very close to each other. She thanked Almighty for everything and went to the kitchen where Tulsibhabhi was preparing breakfast for all. Bimladadi sat on a stool and said "Tulsibhabhi, please prepare our breakfast too. And yes, don't prepare lunch. You all are coming to our house for lunch today. My son will also join us. If God wishes, our dream will come true. Let the boy and the girl meet and talk. If everything goes well, we will take the decision of their marriage as early as possible."

After many months, Chimpu had his breakfast without any dislike. Banno had taken the responsibility to feed him. Both were very happy. When Banno came to know that they were required to go to Bimladadi's house, she immediately asked, "Who is going to cook for us?" Bimladadi replied, "Who else, me?" Banno kept mum for some time and then said, "Ok Aunty, would you mind if I come a bit early to your house and help you to prepare lunch for all of us? Although I am not a good cook, but I can at least help you." Bimladadi could not control herself. She went near Banno, with both her palms took her face and kissed Banno's forehead and said, "I pray to God to bestow all the happiness on you, my child." There were tears in her eyes and she did not hide that.

After some time, they all started for Bimladadi's house. Kantilal had already left for his shop. Chimpu once again became busy with his new red car. This time Tulsibhabhi became his partner in play. Banno and Bimladadi went to the kitchen. Banno took some time to organize the kitchen, and then arranged all the ingredients required for preparing the lunch. The menu was decided with mutual consent. Banno added one more item, "Kofta",to the menu. She was quite an efficient cook. Though she had come here to help, she cooked almost everything herself. A few times, she asked Bimladadi to help. Two of the three hurdles had been crossed. Chimpu and the kitchen had been conquered. The last hurdle was Kantilal. It was almost lunch time. Banno took the initiative to arrange the dining table. She had already prepared two more items, which were green salad and roasted papad. There was a knock at the door. Bimladadi asked Banno to open the door. Hesitatingly, Banno went and slowly opened the door and there he was standing, a handsome gentleman. Both saw each other. Both knew who they were. With folded hands Banno greeted Kantilal. He reciprocated her greeting. They both smiled. Banno asked him to come inside and proceeded towards the dining table. After freshening up, Kantilal came to the dining table where everybody was waiting for him. Kantilal took his designated seat. Chimpu sat next to him on the left side. On the right side, Tulsibhabhi sat. Banno and Bimladadi were to serve the lunch. All were mum. Chimpu was the first to break the silence. He excitedly told his father, "Papa, do you remember that yesterday I told you that I got my fairy friend. Let me show you who she is." Chimpu came down from his seat, went running to Banno, held her hand and brought her near his father. "Here she is, my fairy friend. Dadi brought her for me. She loves me very much. I shall not leave her. I have asked Dadi that my fairy friend should stay in our house. Papa, please, you too tell her to stay here." Kantilal was staring at Banno. She was quite a beautiful girl. One thing she had proven was that she was a magician. In no time, she had mesmerized Shantilal. Even she had given his son a pet name, Chimpu. How sweet! When his wife had died, Shantilal was only two and a half years old. Before the little boy knew his mother well, she was gone. The last six months he was searching frantically for somebody like his mother. Almighty God had listened to his cry and sent this magician as his fairy friend. Though it would be impossible for Kantilal to forget his wife whom he loved so much, he would give their life a chance. If this girl were ready to be a part of this house, he would have no objection. If his son were happy, all would be happy. After their lunch, Tulsibhabhi advised that Banno and Kantilal should sit for some time together to get to know each other. Bimladadi and Tulsibhabhi took Chimpu with them and left that dining space for the two to talk.

Kantilal started the conversation, "Look Banno, without much ado let me clarify my position to you so that you do not have any complaint in the future that I did not tell you. You know I lost my wife. She was very close to me and my son. We were a happy family before the lightning struck our head and my wife was diagnosed with blood cancer. It was already in an advanced stage when we came to know about it. Doctors said she must have realized that something was seriously wrong, but she did not let us know anything. She had hidden the truth of her pain and agony. When the actual treatment started, it was already too late, and the doctors could do little to save her. Ultimately, we lost her, and my son lost his mother who was so close to him. I had decided not to think about remarriage. But for the last six months my son has suffered mentally and psychologically a lot. He has found his mother in you. All the credit goes to you, I must say. I know everything about you. Tulsibhabhi has repeatedly asked me to see you at least once. I had given a condition expecting that my son will not accept anybody as his mother so soon. But you have done a miracle which nobody will deny. So, I have decided that if you feel that I too can be your friend, then I want to marry you without wasting time, so that your Chimpu gets his mother in this house."

Banno replied quietly, "Thank you for accepting me as your friend and Chimpu's mother. For the last five years, I was known as a Bad Omen woman in our society. Despite that you have agreed to marry me and give me back my own pride. Being a woman, it was not difficult for me to be close with Chimpu because I was mentally prepared. I knew that only if I genuinely love Chimpu, only if he truly accepts me as his fairy friend, only then will I be his mother in a real sense. It is a challenge for me to make Chimpu believe that he now has somebody on whom he can depend, can ask her to be his play mate, can quarrel with her and can shout at her if a demand is not fulfilled. I shall try my best to fulfill all his aspirations as any other mother. Most importantly, I will see that he is not spoilt with excess love and affection. Chimpu should grow as a person for whom the society should feel proud including you and me." Smiling, Banno concluded, "Let both of us take a decision to have full faith in each other and along with Chimpu and aunty make this house a beautiful place to live."

Epilogue: Chimpu was an IITian with a high salaried job in the US. Kantilal, Banno, their daughter Chutki and Bimladadi had come to the US for Chutki's admission in MIT. Chimpu was managing everything. Bimladadi's wish had been fulfilled.

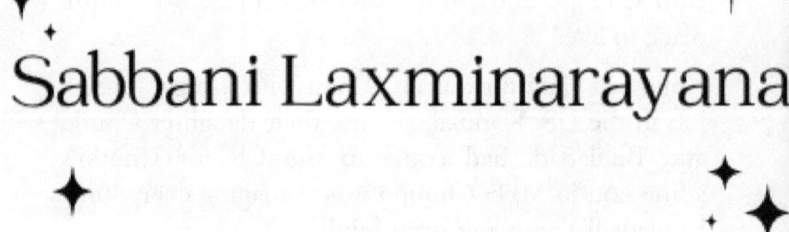

The Journey of Life

1st April 2040, Karimnagar, India.

That day is the 80th birthday of famous writer Narayan. It is a great thing for him to live eighty long years smoothly. Many of his relatives, friends, disciples, fellow poets and writers attended his birthday party. They felicitated him in a grand manner. From America his elder son, daughter- in - law and grandchildren conveyed their wishes to Narayan. Narayan has been writing since the age of twenty years. His literary career spanned over sixty years. Looking back, he achieved more than he wanted. Perhaps it can be said that he had achieved all that he set out to do. Eighty years ago, he was born in a poor family and gradually grew up and became rich. He never traveled with greedy expectations in his life, he never expected anything beyond what he deserves. He is a man who believes that if you work hard, you will surely get success. When he was twenty years old while studying for his degree, he dreamed of becoming a government teacher. He had some ambitions like having a car, constructing a building and becoming a great writer. In his teenage days he thought that after getting a job and getting married, he would have two sons, one son would be named Sarath after his favorite Indian novelist Sarath

Chandra Chattopadhyaya of Bengal and the second son would be named Vamshi Krishna after his favorite novelist Latha the great novelist of Telugu and her novel 'Mohana Vamshi'. He dreamed of establishing a literary and cultural organization named 'Sarath Sahiti Kala Saravanti' in the name of Sarath, the famous Indian novelist.

According to his wish, he completed his three year degree course and after that one year bachelor of education course. After that he got a job as a government teacher. He got married one year after joining the job. A son was born the next year and he was named Sarath. Another son was born four years later, and he named that son Vamsi Krishna. He never stopped his studies. He got Master's Degree in English Literature, Master's Degree in Hindi Literature, Master's Degree in Psychology, Master's Degree in Astrology, Master's Degree in Education as a continuing student. In the sixteenth year of his employment, he built his dream building in the center of the town in the district headquarters. Children grew up and completed their studies. His desire to buy a car also came true in another five years. In another five years he purchased two acres of agricultural land in his hometown. Besides his teaching profession his favorite hobby is reading and writing. He became a bookworm and became a good writer also. Narayan never looked back. By the time he retired from the job, he had published thirty-six books. The fame of his name has spread in the known land of Telugu, even in the country and abroad. He delivered speeches and got felicitation in the two Telugu states of Andhra Pradesh and Telangana at Tirupati, Anantapur, Kadapa, Machilipatnam, Vijayawada, Anakapalli, Hyderabad, Karimnagar, Jagityal. In India at Bengaluru, Udaipur, Bhubaneswar and Calcutta. In America Dallas, Houston, Austin.

Eldest son Sarath settled in America as a software engineer and also built a house there. He had two sons. Grandchildren are US citizens by birth. His eldest son and daughter-in-law got green cards. He went to America twice with his wife. Younger son Vamsi is married and has a son and a daughter. Staying at home, he looks after agriculture, poultry, dairy and business affairs.

His wife Sharada, who is eight years younger than him is a pious woman. Being a good writer Narayan has written more than sixty books in his literary career of sixty years. On the occasion of his retirement at the age of fifty-eight, a souvenir came on him with the writings of his friends and scholars. At the age of sixty years, there was no scope of celebrating his sixtieth birthday (Shasti Poorthi) in 2020. The terrible corona disease shook the whole world. All over the world, airplanes were stopped, trains were stopped, buses were stopped. Roads are empty, bazaars are empty. Shops, offices closed. Life became frozen as a stand still picture. Nowhere To go. Only emergency services of health department personnel, milk vans, vegetable vans and personnel allowed with permission on the roads only in the morning session. In India, a total curfew was enforced across the country on March 22. A nationwide lockdown has been announced from March 23. So the lockdown was imposed till the month of June. People had to live in their houses only. India has conquered the corona by finding a vaccine for Covid within ten months.

From his childhood Narayan was a good student. He has no literary background for him. At the intermediate level he didn't have the literary taste. But accidentally he fell into the ocean of literature. For whom he had written in the early days at the age of twenty years. He wrote for the sake of a beautiful girl he loved dearly in those days! She is now seventy eight years old. She is a good friend of Narayan. She is the cause and inspiration for his writing. He sent her the feelings of his mind by closing his eyes by remembering her. She happily received his feelings and expressed her happiness and appeared on the cellphone screen. She conveyed ' ' Happy Birthday " greetings to Narayan. She congratulated him on his 80th birthday.

Narayan sang a rubai for her.

"Tell me what is in life tell me

What's left for us dear tell me

Time is passing as melting of snow

What else is in life dear tell me "

She smiled and said goodbye while listening to the Rubai and disappeared suddenly from the cell phone screen. Narayan thought that we could not understand the hearts of these ladies. When could they appear and talk and when could they disappear and be silent.

On his 80th birthday, Narayan started writing his autobiography, 'The Journey of Life'. There is no pen and paper like before, there is no such thing as writing on a cell phone. If we put a chip on our head and turn on the cell phone, all our thoughts will be typed directly on the cell phone screen. Our feelings would go directly into apps like Facebook and WhatsApp, thousands and millions of responses would come within seconds and minutes. Everything is the internet world. Narayan did the same. All his feelings are automatically translated into different languages. Over a million readers in the online world read his writings. Now there is no need to cry for the name and fame. Recognition, respect, response we get in seconds!

Really life is a journey. How wonderful it is ! Born in the poorest of the poor family in a small village in the Deccan land of India. Except him all are illiterates in his family. Father died at the age of six. Mother took care of him. She was the poorest mother, she was wise and brave. She lived 86 long years with good health. Narayan wrote an elegy on her death,' Avva, The Mother '. That book was translated into French and Japanese languages. It is the little biography of Narayan. His life reflects in that small book.

Narayan writes in English and Hindi besides his mother tongue Telugu. That brought him good friends from all over India and abroad.

He is just reminiscing about his life……. Childhood, family, parents, education, love, friendship, job, marriage, children, writing, visiting different places and persons… bundle of experiences flowing from his thoughts. That is the Journey of life of Narayan.

Romita Sahni

The hues of pink and red light of "Red Velvet club", aesthetically reflected Amelia's curves, swaying like bougainvillea flowers in cool breezy air. The soft pulsating light enhanced her enchanting silhouette, like a work of art, attracting sheath glances from the crowded dance floor. Her presence had stirred a quiet admiration in the dimly lit corners of the room. Amelia, a renowned makeup artist across the globe, was a huge name in the Fashion industry, with a perfect married life on her social media handles. As she held her glass of martini and strutted across the room to the table encircled by her social butterflies. Her eyes lingered with a mischievous glint, craving to fulfill her unsatisfied desires, an escape from her mundane life. While her husband, a short, stout, middle-aged man, Uzair Sheikh, patiently waited till the wee hours of the morning. Carefully he would put his tipsy wife to her bed, pulling out her heels restricting her beautiful feet to breathe, changing her into comfortable nightwear and lovingly putting her to sleep. He would then draw the curtains and tiptoe to the bathroom to get ready for the tedious job as owner of a popular shoe brand, Stride Rise. Uzair was head over heels for Amelia, oblivious that her mind was consumed elsewhere-the thrill of a new chase, the adrenaline of a new conquest.

She was in a deep slumber. In her dreams, she felt little fingers touching her palm, calling out "Mama".

She could see herself running after a beautiful little girl wearing a pink attire and then she'd vanished in a big hole of cloudy smoke.Amelia woke up in anguish, her eyes watery, hair were in a mess, her head was pounding with pain. She closed her eyes, took a deep breath, and whispered a fervent prayer, "Please bless me with a child. Let me feel whole again." She grabbed her phone, but her eyes froze at the most powerful number 11:11. Was her soul ready for new beginnings and transition? Many people had spoken about the power of the angel numbers. Likewise,she also made a wish at the spiritual hour; she could feel the vibe of goodness around her, as if an angel was whispering in her ear, "You will soon be a mother, Amelia."

It had been 13 years that Uzair and Amelia were married.Love had blossomed amongst them in London where she'd gone for an advance make up course and Uzair was a student of the London School of Economics.Together they'd made a power couple, despite their differences, Amelia and Uzair had complimented each other they never thought possible. They'd first crossed their paths in the Notting Hill Carnival. Their vibe got attracted somewhere between dancing from reggae to the house of Samba. Uzair looked forward to quiet intimate moments with Amelia,away from his boring campus life. Each day brought new challenges, but their love remained steadfast. She smiled, thinking of a good time, and sat up in her bed with a cup of black coffee. She pondered, does marriage make you fall out of love? Or was it after her father-in-law's death, the responsibility of Stride Rise came on Uzair's shoulders? Stride Rise was her husband's dream,he soon wanted to launch the brand in the UAE countries.He'd never doubted Amelia's frivolous actions or her frequent absence.He was busy building his empire,while she slithered into the trap of her dark desires. Each Monday morning she got up with a guilt of being a backstabber, and a nulliparous woman. To take a hold of her life, she submerged herself in work, creating content, taking up makeups, tie ups and collaborations with the premium brands and socializing only with people who had rich connections.

Uzair came back home dog-tired only to find his palatial house deprived of its mistress. All it had was staff buzzing around and taking orders from him. He ordered a ginger honey tea to soothe his itchy throat and to bring relief to the stuffy nose. It seemed difficult for him to breathe. Suddenly, Uzair's body stiffened, his limbs jerked uncontrollably, and his eyes rolled back. A servant leapt to support him until his seizure passed. Amelia was making out wildly at the back of a black limousine, unaware that her world was about to be turned upside down. Uzair had been rushed to the hospital and doctors ran several tests only to reveal a stage four cancer, leaving Amelia devastated. Her world had crumbled around her. She furiously scrubbed her face and wiped out the last traces of make up. She collapsed on her knees, every sob felt like a plea to heaven, questioning why fate had been so unkind to her?

Uzair's health deteriorated, Amelia's fear of losing him grew. She became a victim of her own guilt. Her thoughts again wandered around the 11:11 wish. She adhered to a belief that a child would be the only way to preserve a part of her beloved husband. Uzair rested on his bedside,she held his hand gloomily,he smiled and suggested,"Amy my love,I want to freeze my sperm before starting with the chemo." However, now it seemed impossible as the doctor told her that the cancer treatment can damage sperm health.

As time went by, Amelia's desperation grew, as five of her IVF had failed and Uzair's health deteriorated. The doctor had put Uzair on immune and chemotherapy and, whereas, Amelia panicked as time slipped away swiftly as glass escaped soapy hands. On a shivery cold winter night, Amelia took her pregnancy test. It was her ninth IVF and the 15th day after the insemination procedure.She hurried from her bathroom to the bedroom,revealing the joy of two pink lines.They embraced each other with ecstatic bursts of delight.

Sadly, Uzair had succumbed to a wheelchair as the piercing pain in his bones had become unbearable.He had frequent seizures and numbness.The Chemotherapy had lead to major hair loss and fatigue.As his health deteriorated,Amelia's life was dedicated to the pursuit of her wish.In the following days, Amelia had abandoned the glitterati events, drunken revelry and debauchery. Instead she'd dedicated herself to her husband's health and care. She made sure he had his meals on time, regular check ups and together they went for quiet morning meditation and breathing exercises. The once -high spirited, gung-ho woman had transformed into a shadow of her former self, her eyes constantly haunted with fear of guilt and loss.

Uzair insisted Amelia to visit the factories of Stride Rise and understand the nitty gritties of the shoe industry. She was a quick learner, she'd checked all records, account files and developed healthy relationship with her employees.

Balancing work, doctor's check ups, Uzair's health and her opulent residence had become her everyday life.

After thirteen weeks of pregnancy, it was a day of immense happiness in Uzair and Amelia's life; they were to announce their pregnancy after 14 years of married life. They had got the house decorated, ordered all the staff members to prepare delicacies, and the duo cut a scrumptious Italian cake, Torta Della Nonna, that Amelia had especially baked for Uzair. She offered him a small bite that he successfully swallowed in. "Are you trying to overwhelm me with abundant affection?" he said passionately. Amelia replied somberly, " Wish my love could make you immortal." The moment she said it was 11:11 on her phone's clock. She was about to shut her eyes to ask her most important wish from her angels. But her world had fallen apart, Uzair had left her. He sat in his armchair peacefully. The angels had claimed him.

Amelia navigated the bitter sweet journey of losing her husband and responsibilities of Motherhood. To her, Uzair is holding her hand at the darkest hour. Her daughter's smile had an uncanny resemblance to her father. Amelia had both tears of joy and sorrow mixed when Uzma grinned ear to ear. She had reserved a few videos for Uzma made by her father titled, "My Uzma featuring your dad Uzair." She repeatedly saw those lovely videos, anticipating the time when Uzma could comprehend the love her father had for them.Amelia often felt that a part of them was in heaven, always guiding and making sure of their wellbeing. With each passing day, both Uzma and her husband's brand; Stride Rise grew and flourished.Although Uzair was not by her side, but his memories lived on, in the warmth of their daughter and the legacy of his brand. In the hustle bustle of life, Amelia honored the memories of Uzair by visiting his favorite spots, celebrating his birthday, connecting with his family and friends. Amelia found meaning in raising Uzma and helping her overcome obstacles in life, even if the anguish of her loss persisted in her heart. She promised to be her daughter's mother and father, giving her the support, affection, and direction she required to succeed. They had a kinship that was stronger than words, one that was created in the crucible of hardship and reinforced by their unwavering love for Uzair.Even though she sometimes felt as though she would never be able to cope with his absence, she took solace in the knowledge that his love would always be there for them—like a beacon of hope in the dark.

At 11:11, both morning and night,Amelia would connect with her angels.She knew that he was observing his from the heaven above. Surprisingly, Uzma first uttered words were "Pa", even her first steps were towards her father's portrait.Amelia found comfort in knowing that they were always surrounded by his love.She said a short prayer of gratitude to her angels and Uzair for giving her all the love and the most precious gift,their daughter Uzma, her only reason to live…

Wish at 11:11

Oh,my angels!
Surround me with love and gratitude
Grant me strength,in such magnitude
To fulfill the duties of motherhood
And humbly navigate obstacles in my pursuit

Velmula Jayapal Reddy

As a Witness to Mother's Eyes

Turning the dawn's stage into a nectar lamp,

She, the life's melody, adorns…

Filling every step with the earth's rhythm, holding battles with resilience, And verses with the brightness of lightning,

She stands, a rare pinnacle of vitality,

O woman…

Hiding the darkness of pain in the heart's ocean, Cradling the entire family like a boat, She's the gentle southern breeze of intimacy.

Half the sky she claims, And the earth in patience, Step by step…

She spreads the umbrella of motherhood. Whether spoken or unspoken, she remains the eternal stream of life,

The inner beat of the drum…

Competing with time, To the dawn's chirping, she adds an undying friendship, The undiminished glow of spiritual radiance,

A fresh vibration of the soil.

With showers of praise,

Hymns of comparisons,

And the music of words,

The day doesn't just pass…

Scriptures, prayers, Mantras, devotional songs… In everything, a woman holds a wondrous place.

But how long shall we tolerate the customs of fetal destruction,

The treacherous thoughts of dowry,

The unyielding societal norms?

As a witness to the tearful mother's eyes,

Melt and fulfill all your dreams,

As the bright half of your heart,

Remain, O man!

Not a fragile vine to fall for mere words of praise,
She's not a delicate woman…

Don't pull her courage to the test,

Don't turn her into a calamity by mistake,

Don't invite trouble lightly.

About the Authors

Juju's Pearls (Dr. Reemanshu Bansal)

Juju's Pearls (Dr. Reemanshu Bansal) versatile individual from New Delhi, India. Radiologist, Author, Blogger, Social activist. Alumnus Tata Memorial Hospital, Mumbai. "Radiologist by Day: Author by Night." Top 10 personalities of the year. Top 10 most loved books of the year Founder: JRC Welfare Society, JRC (Juju's Reader Club), JRC Mobile Library - books on wheels: ignite minds of slum children. Authored 24 books. Ranked high on Amazon hot new sellers. Momsie Popsie Diary series is popular. 25 Literary Awards - Golden Book, Bharat Vibhushan, Suenos Book, Young Adult Book of the Year, Author of the year etc. Available as paperback, e-Book format, Audiobook, multi-language translations. In all book fairs. OTT platforms Goa Film Bazaar have taken interest. Visit *reemanshu.blogspot.com*

Contact: *reemanshu2003@gmail.com*

Riddhima Sen

Riddhima Sen is currently studying comparative Literature at Jadavpur University. She is an author, artist and host.

Rhodesia

Rhodesia is a multifaceted individual—a Filipina physician, past medical professor, past clinical and academic administrator, author, painter, and poet. At the remarkable age of nine, she was celebrated as the Philippines' Youngest Author for compiling an anthology of poems. While presently dedicated to being a loving mother of two, she continues to contribute to the well-being of others through teleconsultations, all the while reigniting her passion for the written word.

Purnima Dixit

Purnima a writer by heart...with thoughts in mind and words on paper, inking emotions through her writings. A writer with passion for simplicity, loves to express her emotions, experiences, and opinions about anything that fascinates her. The world of writing inspires & interests her to paint pictures with words. A literature post-graduate, she has always been an avid reader, which inspired her to start writing. From simply writing reviews of few TV episodes on WordPress, she moved to pen down fictional stories, gradually she developed interest in writing poems, She has been writing since 2015 and desires to follow her passion as Writer. When not writing, you can find her listening to good music, Reading and most importantly watching Korean dramas.

Dr Yogesh A Gupta

Dr. Yogesh Gupta is a distinguished senior physician, renowned for his expertise and compassion in healthcare. Beyond medicine, he's a fervent reader and prolific writer, having authored three books and numerous captivating short stories. For Dr. Gupta, books are more than mere words on paper; they're vessels of expression and repositories of history, never to be eradicated. His belief in the enduring power of literature reflects his profound understanding of the human experience. Through his writings, he aspires to immortalize thoughts, ideas, and emotions, fostering a legacy that transcends time and space.

Sanjai Banerji

Sanjai Banerji is an ultra-marathoner, certified mountaineer and Author of four books, Crossing the Finish Line (Running), The Mountaineering Handbook (Mountaineering), Nobody Dies Tonight (Fitness in the Covid-19 Pandemic), a novel Justice on the Hills (Based on a fictional account of Gorkhaland) and two short stories 'Guardians of Nathu La' and 'Krishna's Quest for Kilimanjaro with his Team' published in two anthologies. He recently became at 64 years on 7th March 2024, the oldest Indian with four medical conditions to summit the highest point of the African Continent at Mount Kilimanjaro (Uhuru Peak) 19,341 feet. Sanjai Banerji has a B.Sc (Zoology) and MBA (Production) and is a gold medalist in journalism with 36 years of experience in the steel, paper, and cement sectors.

Dr.Renuka K.P.

Mrs. Renuka K.P. a retired Tahsildar is a native of Ernakulam district in Kerala state. as the daughter of Mr.Parameswaran Paravur (late)and Mrs. Kousalia (late). After her retirement, she spent time as a blogger on social media. She has a YouTube channel. She has published two story books in English and one in Malayalam. She has also written stories in the anthologies 'Chanakya Suthrani', 'Sweet Sixteen 'and 'the character sketch' with tiny tales. She has received several recognitions for her writings.Recently WCEPC has awarded an Honorary Doctorate in Literature with their membership.

Ishita Bagchi

Ishita is a full time public policy and gender rights enthusiast and a part time poet who loves to crack the lamest jokes and is obsessed with coffee. She is also a published writer who has contributed to multiple anthologies and has also written a book titled, "An Overthinker's Journal" which is a collection of poetry published by Umiyoto Publishing House. When not writing or working, you can find her playing the role of a chatterbox quite happily.

Kamalika Bhattacharya

Kamalika Bhattacharya has authored poems, short stories, and editorials for a number of journals. Her work deftly combines passion, drama, and love. She has years of valuable professional experience and has worked for a variety of print and media companies. Her urge to travel motivates her to write down her thoughts and develop a range of storylines. She strives to communicate the gamut of emotions that exist in human life by providing the characters appropriate intonations.

Aurobindo Ghosh

Dr. Aurobindo Ghosh, a versatile figure, holds multiple degrees in Statistics and Economics. After a 35-year teaching career, he became a principal in various management institutions. A motivational speaker and national trainer, he's impacted thousands through NGOs and universities. At 65, he began writing poems and creating paintings, inspired by Indian culture and classical music. Multilingual, he writes poems and short stories in English, Bengali, Hindi, Gujarati, and Marathi. His works include "Lily on the Northern Sky," "Insight Outsight," "Mejoder Golpo," and "Chhondo Hole Mondo Ki." At 75, he remains active, guiding Ph.D. students and publishing research papers. Projects include an audio version of "Insight Outsight" and a collection of Hindi poems.

Sabbani Laxminarayana

Sabbani Laxminarayana, a retired Junior Lecturer in English from Telangana, boasts an impressive literary career with 35 published books in Telugu, spanning poetry, fiction, nonfiction, and prose. He writes in Telugu, Hindi and English. Some of his stories and poems have been translated into English and Hindi languages. Recognized for his academic and literary contributions, he has received awards such as the Best Teacher Award from the Government of Andhra Pradesh in 2013, P.S. Telugu University Award in 2018, and the "Nava Srujan Kala Praveen Award" Kanpur, U.P. in 2020. His patriotic contribution earned him the "Azadi ka Amrit Mahotsav" Desh Bhakti Geet State level Second Prize in 2022 for Telangana State. Acknowledged by the Telangana Book of Records with the "Best Writer Award" in 2023. He has authored 11 books and composed 6 songs on Telangana. For inquiries, Sabbani Laxminarayana can be contacted via email at In.sabbani@gmail.com.

Romita Sahni

Romita Khurana Sahni is an author. She has written many short stories about her experiences from different walks of life. She writes under her pen name of 'Solicitoussoul'. Her blog is read by readers from all over the world. Her book "Solicitoussoul-a collection of soulful short stories was released on 1st January 2022. Lately, her short story "The Sinister Tree" has been released in an anthology of Supernatural Romance. A voracious reader herself, she curated a group of ladies called 'Avidreadersclubdelhi' in April 2019. Her club now comprises of ladies from affluent backgrounds. She has not only inspired the adults but also numerous children to adapt the habit of reading. She's also the founder of 'Avidreadersclub for Kids' from the age of six to sixteen. During pandemic, she taught many children online from Mumbai, Delhi, Kolkata, Dehradun, Assam, Gorakhpur and so on. She is now one of the panelist on CNBC Awaaz for several discussions. She is also hosting a show for children on the historical places of Delhi-Indraprastha -"ateet ki ek adhbudh yatra" which is also curated by her for Disha TV. Currently the Head of the Marketing Communications in News Maker Media.

Velmula Jayapal Reddy

Jayapal Reddy has written poems and songs in Hindi, English and Telugu. Vijay geeth is the patriotic song written by him for the students. The name of the book written by him is Malaya Sameeram. His poems have been printed in yojsna, paala pitta, Nava Telangana and Sahithi Kiranam.

5

www.ingramcontent.com/pod-product-compliance
Lightning Source LLC
LaVergne TN
LVHW041847070526
838199LV00045BA/1486